Nolly Hooker

Page 69
76
118   Jol
136
125

O

SHAKESPEARE'S

THE TEMPEST.

WITH

INTRODUCTION, AND NOTES EXPLANATORY AND CRITICAL.

FOR USE IN SCHOOLS AND CLASSES.

BY THE

REV. HENRY N. HUDSON, LL.D.

———————

BOSTON, U.S.A.:

PUBLISHED BY GINN & COMPANY.

1889.

Entered according to Act of Congress, in the year 1879, by
HENRY N. HUDSON,
In the Office of the Librarian of Congress, at Washington.

Nolly Hooker

Page 69
76
118   Jol
136
125

characters, the doing so in this case would infer such a degree of self-exultation as, it seems to me, his native and habitual modesty would scarce permit.

Source of the Plot.

Shakespeare was so unconscious of his great inventive faculty, so unambitious of originality in his plots and materials, and so apt to found his plays upon some popular chronicle or tale or romance, that he is generally, perhaps justly, presumed to have done so in this instance. Yet no play or novel has been identified as having furnished, in any sort, the basis of *The Tempest*, or any materials towards the composition. Commentators have been very diligent and inquisitive in the search; still, for aught appears thus far, the probability is, that, in this case, the plot had its origin in the Poet's mind. Collins the poet, indeed, told Thomas Warton that he had met with a novel called *Aurelio and Isabella*, dated 1588, and printed in Italian, Spanish, French, and English, upon which he thought *The Tempest* to have been founded : but poor Collins was at the time suffering under his mental disorder ; and, as regards the particular novel he mentioned, his memory must have been at fault; for the story of Aurelio and Isabella has nothing in common with the play.

In the year 1841, however, Mr. Thoms called attention, in *The New Monthly Magazine*, to some remarkable coincidences between *The Tempest* and a German dramatic piece entitled *The Beautiful Sidea*, composed by Jacob Ayrer, who was a notary of Nuremberg, and contemporary with Shakespeare. In this piece, Prince Ludolph and Prince Leudegast answer to Prospero and Alonso. Ludolph is a magician, has an only daughter, Sidea, and an attendant spirit, Runcifal, who has

some points of resemblance to Ariel. Soon after the opening
of the piece, Ludolph, having been vanquished by his rival,
and with his daughter driven into a forest, rebukes her for
complaining of their change of fortune ; and then summons
his spirit Runcifal, in order to learn from him their future
destiny, and their prospects of revenge. Runcifal, who, like
Ariel, is somewhat "moody," announces to Ludolph that the
son of his enemy will shortly become his prisoner. After a
comic episode, Prince Leudegast, with his son Engelbrecht
and the counsellors, is seen hunting in the same forest, when
Engelbrecht and his companion Famulus, having separated
from their associates, are suddenly encountered by Ludolph
and his daughter. He commands them to yield themselves
prisoners ; they refuse, and attempt to draw their swords,
when he renders them powerless by a touch of his magical
wand, and gives Engelbrecht over to Sidea, to carry logs of
wood for her, and to obey her in all things. Later in the
piece, Sidea, moved with pity for the prince's labour in car-
rying logs, declares that she would "feel great joy, if he
would prove faithful to me, and take me in wedlock " ; an
event which is at last happily brought to pass, and leads to a
reconciliation of their parents.

Here the resemblances are evidently much too close to
have been accidental : either the German must have borrowed from Shakespeare, or Shakespeare from the German,
or both of them from some common source. Tieck gave it
as his opinion that the German was derived from an English
original now lost, to which Shakespeare was also indebted
for the incidents of *The Tempest*. There the matter has to
rest for the present. — There is, besides, an old ballad called
The Inchanted Island, which was once thought to have con-
tributed   wards the play : but it is now generally

held to be more modern than the play, and probably founded upon it; the names and some of the incidents being varied, as if on purpose to disguise its connection with a work that was popular on the stage.

Locality of the Scene.

There has been considerable discussion as to the scene of *The Tempest*. A wide range of critics from Mr Chalmers to Mrs. Jameson have taken for granted that the Poet fixed his scene in the Bermudas. For this they have alleged no authority but his mention of "the still-vex'd Bermoothes." Ariel's trip from "the deep nook to fetch dew from the still-vex'd Bermoothes" does indeed show that the Bermudas were in the Poet's mind; but then it also shows that his scene was not there; for it had been no feat at all worth mentioning for Ariel to fetch dew from one part of the Bermudas to another. An aerial voyage of some two or three thousand miles was the least that so nimble a messenger could be expected to make any account of. Besides, in less than an hour after the wrecking of the King's ship, the rest of the fleet are said to be upon the Mediterranean, "bound sadly home for Naples." On the other hand, the Rev. Mr. Hunter is very positive that, if we read the play with a map before us, we shall bring up at the island of Lampedusa, which "lies midway between Malta and the African coast." He makes out a pretty fair case, nevertheless I must be excused; not so much that I positively reject his theory as that I simply do not care whether it be true or not. But, if we must have any supposal about it, the most reasonable as well as the most poetical one seems to be, that the Poet, writing without a map, placed his scene upon an island of the mind; and that it suited his purpose to transfer to his

ideal whereabout some of the wonders of Transatlantic discovery. I should almost as soon think of going to history
for the characters of Ariel and Caliban, as to geography for
the size, locality, or whatsoever else, of their dwelling-place.
And it is to be noted that the old ballad just referred to
seems to take for granted that the island was but an island
of the mind; representing it to have disappeared upon Prospero's leaving it : —

> From that day forth the isle has been
> By wandering sailors never seen :
> Some say 'tis buried deep
> Beneath the sea, which breaks and roars
> Above its savage rocky shores,
> Nor e'er is known to sleep.

General Characteristics.

The Tempest is on all hands regarded as one of Shake-
peare's perfectest works. Some of his plays, I should say,
have beams in their eyes; but this has hardly so much as a
mote; or, if it have any motes, my own eyes are not clear
enough to discern them. I dare not pronounce the work
faultless, for this is too much to affirm of any human workmanship; but I venture to think that whatever faults it may
have are such as criticism is hardly
In the characters of Ariel, Miranda,
three of the most unique and origin
sprang from the wit of man
the Ideal could be push
here find it clothed wi
And the whole texture
in keeping with that I
lars cohere together,

The leading sentiment naturally inspired by the scenes of this drama is, I believe, that of delighted wonder. And such, as appears from the heroine's name, Miranda, who is *the* potency of the drama, is probably the sentiment which the play was meant to inspire. But the grace and efficacy in which the workmanship is steeped are so etherial and so fine, that they can hardly be discoursed in any but the poetic form : it may well be doubted whether Criticism has any fingers delicate enough to grasp them. So much is this the case, that it seemed to me quite doubtful whether I should do well to undertake the theme at all. For Criticism is necessarily obliged to substitute, more or less, the forms of logic for those of art ; and art, it scarce need be said, can do many things that are altogether beyond the reach of logic. On the other hand, the charm and verdure of these scenes are so unwithering and inexhaustible, that I could not quite make up my mind to leave the subject untried. Nor do I know how I can better serve my countrymen than by engaging and helping them in the study of this great inheritance of natural wisdom and unreproved delight. For, assuredly, if they early learn to be at home and to take pleasure in Shakespeare's workmanship, their whole after-life will be the better and the happier for it.

Coleridge says "*The Tempest* is a specimen of the purely romantic drama." The term *romantic* is here used in a technical sense ; that is, to distinguish the Shakespearian from the Classic Drama. In this sense, I cannot quite agree with the great critic that the drama is *purely* romantic. Highly romantic it certainly is, in its wide, free, bold variety of character and incident, and in all the qualities that enter into the picturesque ; yet not romantic in such sort, I think, but that it is at the same time equally classic ; classic, not only in that the unities of time and place are strictly observed, but as having the other qualities which naturally go with those laws of the classic form ; in its severe beauty and majestic simplicity, its interfusion of the lyrical and ethical, and in the mellow atmosphere of serenity and composure which envelopes it : as if on purpose to show the Poet's mastery not only of both the Classic and Romantic Drama, but of the common Nature out of which both of them grew. This union of both kinds in one without hindrance to the distinctive qualities of either, — this it is, I think, that chiefly distinguishes *The Tempest* from the Poet's other dramas. Some have thought that in this play Shakespeare specially undertook to silence the pedantic cavillers of his time by showing that he could keep to the rules of the Greek stage, if he chose to do so, without being any the less himself. But it seems more likely that he was here drawn into such a course by the leading of his own wise spirit than by the cavils of contemporary critics ; the form appearing too cognate with the matter to have been dictated by any thing external to the work itself.

There are some points that naturally suggest a comparison between *The Tempest* and *A Midsummer-Night's Dream*. In both the Poet has with equal or nearly equal success carried Nature, as it were, beyond herself, and peopled a purely ideal region with the attributes of life and reality ; so that the characters touch us like substantive, personal beings, as if he had but described, not created them. But. beyond this, the resemblance ceases : indeed no two of his plays differ more widely in all other respects.

The Tempest presents a combination of elements apparently so .... not but marvel how they were ...... nd so sweetly, and cöoperate so smoothly, that we at once feel at home with them, and see nothing to hinder their union in the world of which we are a part. For in the mingling of the natural and the supernatural we here find no gap, no break; nothing disjointed or abrupt; the two being drawn into each other so harmoniously, and so knit together by mutual participations, that they seem strictly continuous, with no distinguishable line to mark where they meet and join. It is as if the gulf which apparently separates the two worlds had been abolished, leaving nothing to prevent a free circulation and intercourse between them.

The Hero.

Próspero, standing in the centre of the whole, acts as a kind of subordinate Providence, reconciling the diverse elements to himself and in himself to one another. Though armed with supernatural might, so that the winds and waves obey him, his magical and mysterious powers are tied to truth and right: his " high charms work " to none but just and beneficent ends; and whatever might be repulsive in the magician is softened and made attractive by the virtues of the man and the feelings of the father: Ariel links him with the world above us, Caliban with the world beneath us, and Miranda — " thee, my dear one, thee my daughter " — with the world around and within us. And the mind acquiesces freely in the miracles ascribed to him; his thoughts and aims being so at one with Nature's inward harmonies, that we cannot tell whether he shapes her movements or merely falls in with them; that is, whether his art stands in submission or command. His sorcery indeed is the sorcery of knowledge, his magic the magic of virtue. For what so marvellous as the inward, vital necromancy of good which

transmutes the wrongs that are done him into motives of
beneficence, and is so far from being hurt by the powers of
Evil, that it turns their assaults into new sources of strength
against them? And with what a smooth tranquillity of spirit
he everywhere speaks and acts ! as if the discipline of adver-
sity had but served

> to elevate the will,
> And lead him on to that transcendent rest
> Where every passion doth the sway attest
> Of Reason seated on her sovereign hill.

Shakespeare and Bacon, the Prince of poets and the Prince
of philosophers, wrought out their mighty works side by side,
and nearly at the same time, though without any express
recognition of each other. And why may we not regard
Prospero as prognosticating in a poetical form those vast
triumphs of man's rational spirit which the philosopher fore-
saw and prepared? For it is observable that, before Prospero's coming to the island, the powers which cleave to his
thoughts and obey his " so potent art " were at perpetual
war, the better being in subjection to the worse, and all being
turned from their rightful ends into a mad, brawling dissonance : but he teaches them to know their places ; and,
" weak masters though they be," without such guidance, yet
under his ordering they become powerful, and work together
as if endowed with a rational soul and a social purpose ; their
insane gabble turning to speech, their savage howling to
music ; so that

> the isle is full of noises,
> Sounds, and sweet airs, that give delight, and hurt not.

Wherein is boldly figured the educating of Nature up, so to
speak, into intelligent ministries, she lending man hands because he lends her eyes, and weaving her forces into vital
union with him.

                    You by whose aid —
Weak masters though ye be — I have bedimm'd
The noontide Sun, call'd forth the mutinous winds,
And 'twixt the green sea and the azure vault
Set roaring war: to the dread-rattling thunder
Have I given fire, and rifted Jove's stout oak
With his own bolt: the strong-based promontory
Have I made shake; and by the spurs pluck'd up
The pine and cedar.

In this bold imagery we seem to have a kind of prophecy of what human science and skill have since achieved in taming the great forces of Nature to man's hand, and harnessing them into his service.   Is not all this as if the infernal powers should be appeased and soothed by the melody and sweetness of the Orphean harp and voice?   And do we not see how the very elements themselves grow happy and merry in serving man, when he by his wisdom and eloquence has once charmed them into order and concert?   Man has but to learn Nature's language and obey her voice, and she clothes him with plenipotence.   The mad warring of her forces turns to rational speech and music when he holds the torch of reason before them and makes it shine full in their faces.   Let him but set himself steadfastly to understand and observe her laws, and her mighty energies hasten to wait upon him, as docile to his hand as the lion to the eye and voice of Lady Una.   So that we may not unfairly apply to Prospero what Bacon so finely interprets of Orpheus, as "a wonderful and divine person skilled in all kinds of harmony, subduing and drawing all things after him by sweet and gentle methods and modulations."

All this, to be sure, is making the work rather an allegory than a drama, and therein of course misrepresents its quality. For the connecting links in this strange intercourse of man

and Nature are " beings individually determined," and affect
us as persons, not as propositions.

Prospero's Prime Minister.

Ariel and Caliban are equally preternatural, though in opposite directions. Ariel's very being is spun out of melody
and fragrance ; at least, if a feeling soul and an intelligent
will are the warp, these are the woof of his exquisite texture.
He has just enough of human-heartedness to know how he
would feel were he human, and a proportionable sense of
gratitude, which has been aptly called " the memory of the
heart " : hence he needs to be often reminded of his obligations, but is religiously true to them so long as he remembers
them. His delicacy of nature is nowhere more apparent
than in his sympathy with right and good : the instant he
comes within their touch he follows them without reserve ;
and he will suffer any torments rather than " act the earthy
and abhorr'd commands " that go against his moral grain.
And what a merry little personage he is withal ! as if his
being were cast together in an impulse of play, and he would
spend his whole life in one perpetual frolic.

But the main ingredients of Ariel's zephyr-like constitution
are shown in his leading inclinations ; as he naturally has
most affinity for that of which he is framed. Moral ties are
irksome to him ; they are not his proper element : when he
enters their sphere, he feels them to be holy indeed ; but,
were he free, he would keep out of their reach, and follow
the circling seasons in their course, and always dwell merrily
in the fringes of Summer. Prospero quietly intimates his
instinctive dread of the cold by threatening to make him
" howl away twelve Winters." And the chief joy of his
promised release from service is, that he will then be free

to live all the year through under the soft rule of Summer, with its flowers and fragrancies and melodies. He is indeed an arrant little epicure of perfume and sweet sounds, and gives forth several songs which "seem to sound in the air, and as if the person playing them were invisible."

A part of Ariel's unique texture is well shown in the scene where he relents at the sufferings of the shipwrecked lords, and remonstrates with his master in their behalf : —

> *Ariel.*   The King,
> His brother, and yours, abide all three distracted;
> And the remainder mourning over them,
> Brimful of sorrow and dismay; but chiefly
> He that you term'd *the good old lord, Gonsalo :*
> His tears run down his beard, like winter-drops
> From eaves of reeds. Your charm so strongly works 'em,
> That, if now beheld them, your affections
> Would become tender.
> > *Pros.*   Dost thou think so, spirit ?
> *Ariel.* Mine would, sir, were I human.

Another mark-worthy feature of Ariel is, that his power does not stop with the physical forces of Nature, but reaches also to the hearts and consciences of men ; so that by his music he can kindle or assuage the deepest griefs of the one, and strike the keenest pangs of remorse into the other. This comes out in the different effects of his art upon Ferdinand and the guilty King, as related by the men themselves : —

> Where should this music be ? i' the air or th' earth ?
> It sounds no more: and, sure, it waits upon
> Some god o' the island. Sitting on a bank,
> Weeping again the King my father's wreck,
> This music crept by me upon the waters,
> Allaying both their fury and my passion
> With its sweet air: thence I have follow'd it,
> Or it hath drawn me rather: but 'tis gone.
> No, it begins again.

Such is the effect on Ferdinand : now mark the contrast when we come to the King : —

> O, it is monstrous, monstrous!
> Methought the billows spoke, and told me of it;
> The winds did sing it to me: and the thunder,
> That deep and dreadful organ-pipe, pronounced
> The name of Prosper: it did bass my trespass.
> Therefore my son i' the ooze is bedded; and
> I'll seek him deeper than e'er plummet sounded,
> And with him there lie mudded.

In the planting of love, too, Ariel beats old god Cupid all to nothing. For it is through some witchcraft of his that Ferdinand and Miranda are surprised into a mutual rapture ; so that Prospero notes at once how " at the first sight they have changed eyes," and " are both in either's power." All which is indeed just what Prospero wanted ; yet he is himself fairly startled at the result : that fine issue of nature outruns his thought ; and the wise old gentleman takes care forthwith lest it work too fast : —

> This swift business
> I must uneasy make, lest too light winning
> Make the prize light.

I must note one more trait in Ariel. It is his fondness of mischievous sport, wherein he reminds us somewhat of Fairy Puck in *A Midsummer-Night's Dream*. It is shown in the evident gust with which he relates the trick he has played on Caliban and his confederates, when they were proceeding to execute their conspiracy against the hero's life : —

> As I told you, sir, they were red-hot with drinking;
> So full of valour, that they smote the air
> For breathing in their faces; beat the ground
> For kissing of their feet; yet always bending
> Towards their project. Then I beat my tabor;
> At which, like unback'd colts, they prick'd their ears,

> Advanced their eyelids, lifted up their noses
> As they smelt music: so I charm'd their ears,
> That, calf-like, they my lowing follow'd through
> Tooth'd briers, sharp furzes, pricking goss, and thorns,
> Which enter'd their frail shins: at last I left them
> I' the filthy-mantled pool beyond your cell,
> There dancing up to th' chins.

Of Ariel's powers and functions as Prospero's prime minister, no logical forms, nothing but the Poet's art, can give any sort of an idea. No painter, I am sure, can do any thing with him; still less can any sculptor. Gifted with the ubiquity and multiformity of the substance from which he is named, before we can catch and define him in any one shape, he has passed into another. All we can say of him on this score is, that through his agency Prospero's thoughts forthwith become things, his volitions events. And yet, strangely and diversely as Ariel's nature is elemented and composed, with touches akin to several orders of being, there is such a self-consistency about him, he is so cut out in individual distinctness, and so rounded-in with personal attributes, that contemplation freely and easily rests upon him as an object. In other words, he is by no means an abstract idea personified, or any sort of intellectual diagram, but a veritable *person;* and we have a personal feeling towards the dear creature, and would fain knit him into the living circle of our human affections, making him a familiar playfellow of the heart, to be cherished with " praise, blame, love, kisses, tears, and smiles."

Caliban.

If Caliban strikes us as a more wonderful creation than Ariel, it is probably because he has more in common with us, without being in any proper sense human. Perhaps I cannot hit him off better than by saying that he represents, both in body and soul, a sort of intermediate nature between man and brute, with an infusion of something that belongs to neither; as though one of the transformations imagined by the evolutionists had stuck midway in its course, where a breath or vapour of essential Evil had knit itself vitally into his texture. Caliban has all the attributes of humanity from the moral downwards, so that his nature touches and borders upon the sphere of moral life: still the result but approves his exclusion from such life, in that it brings him to recognize moral law only as making for self; that is, he has intelligence of seeming wrong in what is done to him, but no conscience of what is wrong in his own doings. It is a most singular and significant stroke in the delineation, that sleep seems to loosen the fetters of his soul, and lift him above himself: then indeed, and then only, "the muddy vesture of decay" doth not so "grossly close him in," but that some proper spirit-notices come upon him; as if in his passive state the voice of truth and good vibrated down *to* his soul, and stopped there, being unable to kindle any answering tones within: so that in his waking hours they are to him but as the memory of a dream.

> Sometime a thousand twangling instruments
> Will hum about mine ears; and sometime voices,
> That, if I then had waked after long sleep,
> Will make me sleep again: and then, in dreaming,
> The clouds methought would open, and show riches
> Ready to drop upon me; that, when I waked,
> I cried to dream again.

Thus Caliban is part man, part demon, part brute, each being drawn somewhat out of itself by combination with the others, and the union of all preventing him from being either; for which cause language has no generic term that

fits him.   Yet this strange, uncouth, but life-like confusion of
natures Prospero has educated into a sort of poet.   This,
however, has nowise tamed, it has rather increased, his innate malignity and crookedness of disposition ; education
having of course but *educed* what was in him.   Even his
poetry is, for the most part, made up of the fascinations of
ugliness ; a sort of inverted beauty ; the poetry of dissonance
and deformity ; the proper music of his nature being to
curse, its proper laughter to snarl.   Schlegel finely compares
his mind to a dark cave, into which the light of knowledge
falling neither illuminates nor warms it, but only serves to
put in motion the poisonous vapours generated there.

Now it is by exhausting the resources of instruction on
such a being that his innate and essential deficiency is best
shown.   For, had he the germs of a human soul, they must
needs have been drawn forth by the process that has made
him a poet.   The magical presence of spirits has indeed cast
into the caverns of his brain some faint reflection of a better
world, but without calling up any answering emotions or as-
pirations ; he having no susceptibilities to catch and take in
the epiphanies that throng his whereabout.   So that, para-
doxical as it may seem, he exemplifies the two-fold triumph
of art over nature, and of nature over art ; that is, art has tri-
umphed in making him a poet, and nature, in still keeping
him from being a man ; though he has enough of the human
in him to evince in a high degree the swelling of intellectual
pride.

But what is most remarkable of all in Caliban is the perfect
originality of his thoughts and manners.   Though framed of
grossness and malignity, there is nothing vulgar or common-
place about him.   His whole character indeed is developed
from within, not impressed from without ; the effect of Pros-

pero's instructions having been to make him all the more himself; and there being perhaps no soil in his nature for conventional vices and knaveries to take root and grow in. Hence the almost classic dignity of his behaviour compared with that of the drunken sailors, who are little else than a sort of low, vulgar conventionalities organized, and as such not less true to the life than consistent with themselves. In his simplicity, indeed, he at first mistakes them for gods who " bear celestial liquor," and they wax merry enough at the " credulous monster"; but, in his vigour of thought and purpose, he soon conceives such a scorn of their childish interest in whatever trinkets and gewgaws meet their eye, as fairly drives off his fit of intoxication ; and the savage of the woods, half-human though he be, seems nobility itself beside the savages of the city.

In fine, if Caliban is, so to speak, the organized sediment and dregs of the place, from which all the finer spirit has been drawn off to fashion the delicate Ariel, yet having some parts of a human mind strangely interwoven with his structure ; every thing about him, all that he does and says, is suitable and correspondent to such a constitution of nature. So that all the elements and attributes of his being stand and work together in living coherence, thus rendering him no less substantive and personal to our apprehension than he is original and peculiar in himself.

The Heroine.

Such are the objects and influences amidst which the clear, placid nature of Miranda has been developed. Of the world whence her father was driven, its crimes and follies and sufferings, she knows nothing ; he having studiously kept all such notices from her, to the end, apparently, that nothing might thwart or hinder the plastic efficacies that surrounded her. And here all the simple and original elements of her being, love, light, grace, honour, innocence, all pure feelings and tender sympathies, whatever is sweet and gentle and holy in womanhood, seem to have sprung up in her nature as from celestial seed : " the contagion of the world's slow stain " has not visited her ; the chills and cankers of artificial wisdom have not touched nor come nigh her : if there were any fog or breath of evil in the place that might else dim or spot her soul, it has been sponged up by Caliban, as being more congenial with his nature ; while he is simply " a villain she does not love to look on." Nor is this all.

The aerial music beneath which her nature has expanded with answering sweetness seems to rest visibly upon her, linking her as it were with some superior order of beings : the spirit and genius of the place, its magic and mystery, have breathed their power into her face ; and out of them she has unconsciously woven herself a robe of supernatural grace, in which even her mortal nature seems half hidden, so that we are in doubt whether she belongs more to Heaven or to Earth. Thus both her native virtues and the efficacies of the place seem to have crept and stolen into her unperceived, by mutual attraction and assimilation twining together in one growth, and each diffusing its life and beauty over and through the others. It would seem indeed as if Wordsworth must have had Miranda in his eye, (or was he but working in the spirit of that Nature which she so rarely exemplifies?) when he wrote the following : —

> The floating clouds their state shall lend
> To her ; for her the willow bend ;
>   Nor shall she fail to see

Even in the motions of the storm
Grace that shall mould the maiden's form
  By silent sympathy.

The stars of midnight shall be dear
To her; and she shall lean her ear
  In many a secret place
Where rivulets dance their wayward round,
And beauty born of murmuring sound
  Shall pass into her face.

Yet, for all this, Miranda not a whit the less touches us as a creature of flesh and blood, —

  A being breathing thoughtful breath,
  A traveller between life and death.

Nay, rather she seems all the more so, inasmuch as the character thus coheres with the circumstances, the virtues and poetries of the place being expressed in her visibly; and she would be far less real to our feelings, were not the wonders of her whereabout thus vitally incorporated with her innate and original attributes.

It is observable that Miranda does not perceive the working of her father's art upon herself. For, when he casts a spell of drowsiness over her, so that she cannot choose but sleep, on being awaked by him she tells him, " The strangeness of your story put heaviness in me." So his art conceals itself in its very potency of operation ; and seems the more like nature for being preternatural. It is another noteworthy point, that while he is telling his strange tale he thinks she is not listening attentively to his speech, partly because he is not attending to it himself, his thoughts being busy with the approaching crisis of his fortune, and drawn away to the other matters which he has in hand, and partly because in her trance of wonder at what he is relating she seems abstracted and self-withdrawn from the matter of his discourse.

His own absent-mindedness on this occasion is aptly and artfully indicated by his broken and disjointed manner of speech. That his tongue and thought are not beating time together appears in that the latter end of his sentences keeps forgetting the beginning.

These are among the fine strokes and delicate touches whereby the Poet makes, or rather permits, the character of his persons to transpire so quietly as not to excite special notice at the time. That Miranda should be so rapt at her father's tale as to seem absent and wandering, is a charming instance in point. For indeed to her the supernatural stands in the place of Nature; and nothing is so strange and wonderful as what actually passes in the life and heart of man: miracles have been her daily food, her father being the greatest miracle of all; which must needs make the common events and passions and perturbations of the world seem to her miraculous. All which is wrought out by the Poet with so much art and so little appearance of art, that Franz Horn is the only critic, so far as I know, that seems to have thought of it.

I must not dismiss Miranda without remarking the sweet union of womanly dignity and childlike simplicity in her character, she not knowing or not caring to disguise the innocent movements of her heart. This, too, is a natural result of her situation. The instance to which I refer is when Ferdinand, his manhood all alive with her, lets her hear his soul speak; and she, weeping at what she is glad of, replies,—

> Hence, bashful cunning!
> And prompt me, plain and holy innocence!—
> I am your wife, if you will marry me:
> If not, I'll die your maid: to be your fellow
> You may deny me; but I'll be your servant,
> Whether you will or no.

Equally fine is the circumstance that her father opens to her the story of his life, and lets her into the secret of her noble birth and ancestry, at a time when she is suffering with those that she saw suffer, and when her eyes are jewelled with " drops that sacred pity hath engender'd " ; as if on purpose that the ideas of rank and dignity may sweetly blend and coalesce in her mind with the sympathies of the woman.

The Prince.

In Ferdinand is portrayed one of those happy natures, such as we sometimes meet with, who are built up all the more strongly in truth and good by contact with the vices and meannesses of the world.   Courage, piety, and honour are his leading characteristics ; and these virtues are so much at home in his breast, and have such an easy, natural ascendant in his conduct, that he thinks not of them, and cares only to prevent or remove the stains which affront his inward eye.   The meeting of him and Miranda is replete with magic indeed, — a magic higher and more potent even than Prospero's ; the riches that nestle in their bosoms at once leaping forth and running together in a stream of poetry which no words of mine can describe.   So much of beauty in so few words, and those few so plain and simple, — " O, wondrous skill and sweet wit of the man ! "

Shakespeare's genius is specially venerable in that he makes piety and honour go hand in hand with love.   It seems to have been a fixed principle with him, if indeed it was not rather a genial instinct, that where the heart is rightly engaged, there the highest and tenderest thoughts of religion do naturally cluster and converge.   For indeed the love that looks to marriage is itself a religion : its first impulse is to invest its object with poetry and consecration : to be " true to

the kindred points of Heaven and home," is both its inspiration and its law. It thus involves a sort of regeneration of the
inner man, and carries in its hand the baptismal fire of a
nobler and diviner life.

And so it is in this delectable instance. In Ferdinand, as
in all generous natures, "love betters what is best." Its first
springing in his breast stirs his heavenward thoughts and as-
pirations into exercise : the moment that kindles his heart
towards Miranda also kindles his soul in piety to God ; and
he knows not how to commune in prayer with the Source of
good, unless he may couple her welfare with his own, and
breathe her name in his holiest service. Thus his love and
piety are kindred and coefficient forces, as indeed all true
love and piety essentially are. However thoughtless we may
be of the Divine help and guardianship for ourselves, we can
hardly choose but crave them for those to whom our souls
are knit in the sacred dearness of household ties. And so
with this noble pair, the same power that binds them to each
other in the sacraments of love also binds them both in de-
vout allegiance to the Author of their being ; whose presence is most felt by them in the sacredness of their mutual
truth.

So much for the illustration here so sweetly given of the
old principle, that whatsoever lies nearest a Christian's heart,
whatsoever he tenders most dearly on Earth, whatsoever
draws in most intimately with the currents of his soul, that
is the spontaneous subject-matter of his prayers ; our purest
loves thus sending us to God, as if from an instinctive feeling that, unless God be sanctified in our hearts, our hearts
cannot retain their proper life.

In regard to what springs up between Ferdinand and Miranda, it is to be noted that Prospero does little but furnish

occasions. He indeed thanks the quaint and delicate Ariel for the kindling touch that so quickly puts them "both in either's power"; for it seems to him the result of a finer inspiration than his art can reach; and so he naturally attributes it to the magic of his airy minister; whereas in truth it springs from a source far deeper than the magic of either, —a pre-established harmony which the mutual recognition now first quickens into audible music. After seeing himself thus outdone by the Nature he has been wont to control, and having witnessed such a "fair encounter of two most rare affections," no wonder that Prospero longs to be a man again, like other men, and gladly returns to

> The homely sympathy that heeds
> The common life, our nature breeds;
> A wisdom fitted to the needs
> Of hearts at leisure.

Antonio, Sebastian, and Gonzalo.

The strength and delicacy of imagination displayed in the characters already noticed are hardly more admirable than the truth and subtilty of observation shown in others.

In the delineation of Antonio and Sebastian, short as it is, we have a volume of wise science, which Coleridge remarks upon thus: "In the first scene of the second Act, Shakespeare has shown the tendency in bad men to indulge in scorn and contemptuous expressions, as a mode of getting rid of their own uneasy feelings of inferiority to the good, and also of rendering the transition of others to wicknedness easy, by making the good ridiculous. Shakespeare never puts habitual scorn into the mouths of other than bad men, as here in the instance of Antonio and Sebastian."

Nor is there less of judgment in the means used by Prospero

for bringing them to a better mind; provoking in them the
purpose of crime, and then taking away the performance;
that so he may lead them to a knowledge of themselves,
and awe or shame down their evil by his demonstrations
of good. For such is the proper effect of bad designs thus
thwarted, showing the authors at once the wickedness of
their hearts and the weakness of their hands; whereas, if
successful in their schemes, pride of power would forestall
and prevent the natural shame and remorse of guilt. And
we little know what evil it lieth and lurketh in our hearts to
will or to do, till occasion invites or permits; and Prospero's
art here stands in presenting the occasion till the wicked
purpose is formed, and then removing it as soon as the hand
is raised. In the case of Antonio and Sebastian, the work-
ings of magic are so mixed up with those of Nature, that we
cannot distinguish them; or rather Prospero here causes
the supernatural to pursue the methods of Nature.

And the same deep skill is shown in the case of the good
old Lord Gonzalo, whose sense of his own infelicities seems
lost in his care to minister comfort and diversion to others.
Thus his virtue spontaneously opens the springs of wit and
humour in him amid the terrors of the storm and shipwreck;
and he is merry while others are suffering, and merry even
from sympathy with them; and afterwards his thoughtful
spirit plays with Utopian fancies; and if "the latter end of
his Commonwealth forgets the beginning," it is all the same
to him, his purpose being only to beguile the anguish of
supposed bereavement. It has been well said that "Gonzalo is so occupied with duty, in which alone he finds pleasure, that he scarce notices the gnat-stings of wit with which
his opponents pursue him; or, if he observes, firmly and
easily repels them."

The Comic Matter.

The comic portions and characters of this play are in Shakespeare's raciest vein; yet they are perfectly unique and singular withal, being quite unlike any other of his preparations in that kind, as much so as if they were the growth of a different planet.

The presence of Trinculo and Stephano in the play has sometimes been regarded as a blemish. I cannot think it so. Their part is not only good in itself as comedy, but is in admirable keeping with the rest. Their follies give a zest and relish to the high poetries amidst which they grow. Such things go to make up the mysterious whole of human life; and they often help on our pleasure while seeming to hinder it: we may think they were better left out, but, were they left out, we should somehow feel the want of them. Besides, this part of the work, if it does not directly yield a grateful fragrance, is vitally connected with the parts that do. For there is perhaps no one of the Poet's dramas of which it can be more justly affirmed that all the parts draw together in organic unity, so that every thing helps every other thing.

Concluding Remarks.

Such are the strangely-assorted characters that make up this charming play. This harmonious working together of diverse and opposite elements, — this smooth concurrence of heterogeneous materials in one varied yet coherent impression, — by what subtile process this is brought about, is perhaps too deep a problem for Criticism to solve.

I cannot leave the theme without remarking what an atmosphere of wonde͏̈   hangs and pervades this singular structure; and how the whole seems steeped in glories invisible to the natural eye, yet made visible by the Poet's art: so that the effect is to lead the thoughts insensibly upwards to other worlds and other forms of being. It were difficult to name any thing else of human workmanship so thoroughly transfigured with

> the gleam,
> The light that never was on sea or land,
> The consecration and the poet's dream.

The celestial and the earthly are here so commingled, — commingled, but not confounded, — that we see not where the one begins or the other ends: so that in the reading we seem transported to a region where we are strangers, yet old acquaintances; where all things are at once new and familiar; the unearthly visions of the spot hardly touching us with surprise, because, though wonderful indeed, there is nothing about them but what readily finds or creates some answering powers and sympathies within us. In other words, they do not surprise us, because they at once kindle us into fellowship with them. That our thoughts and feelings are thus at home with such things, and take pleasure in them, — is not this because of some innate aptitudes and affinities of our nature for a supernatural and celestial life?

> Point not these mysteries to an art
> Lodged above the starry pole?—

Professor Dowden's Comments.

The wrong-doers of *The Tempest* are a group of persons of various degrees of criminality, from Prospero's perfidious brother, still active in plotting evil, to Alonso, whose obligations to the Duke of Milan had been of a public or princely kind. Spiritual powers are in alliance with Prospero; and

these, by terror and the awakening of remorse, prepare Alonso
for receiving the balm of Prospero's forgiveness. He looks
upon his son as lost, and recognizes in his son's loss the pun-
ishment of his own guilt. " The powers delaying, not forgetting," have incensed the sea and shores against the sinful
men ; nothing can deliver them except " heart-sorrow, and
a clear life ensuing." Goethe, in the opening of the Second
Part of *Faust*, has represented the ministry of external nature
fulfilling functions with reference to the human conscience
precisely the reverse of those ascribed to it in *The Tempest*.
Faust, escaped from the prison-scene and the madness of
Margarete, is lying on a flowery grass-plot, weary, restless,
striving to sleep. The Ariel of Goethe calls upon his attendant elvish spirits to prepare the soul of Faust for renewed
energy by bathing him in the dew of Lethe's stream, by
assuaging his pain, by driving back remorse. To dismiss
from his conscience the sense of the wrong he has done to
a dead woman, is the initial step in the further education
and development of Faust. Shakespeare's Ariel, breathing
through the elements and the powers of Nature, quickens
the remorse of the King for a crime of twelve years since.

The enemies of Prospero are now completely in his power.
How shall he deal with them? They had perfidiously taken
advantage of his unworldly and unpractical habits of life ;
they had thrust him away from his dukedom ; they had
exposed him with his three-years'-old daughter in a rotten
boat to the mercy of the waves. Shall he not now avenge
himself without remorse? What is Prospero's decision?

> Though with their high wrongs I am struck to th' quick,
> Yet with my nobler reason 'gainst my fury
> Do I take part: the rarer action is
> In virtue than in vengeance: they being penitent,
> The sole drift of my purpose doth extend
> Not a frown further.

We have seen how Timon turned fiercely upon mankind, and hated the wicked race : " I am Misanthropos, and hate mankind." The wrongs inflicted upon Prospero were crueller and more base than those from which Timon suffered. But Prospero had not lived in a summer mood of lax and prodigal benevolence : he had lived severely, " all dedicated to closeness and the bettering of my mind." And out of the strong comes forth sweetness. In the play of *Cymbeline*, the wrong which Posthumus has suffered from the Italian Iachimo is only less than that which Othello endures at the hands of Iago. But Iachimo, unlike Iago, is unable to sustain the burden of his guilt, and sinks under it. In the closing scene of *Cymbeline*, that in which Posthumus is himself welcomed home to the heart of Imogen, Posthumus in his turn becomes the pardoner : —

> Kneel not to me :
> The power that I have on you is to spare you ;
> The malice toward you to forgive you : live,
> And deal with others better.

Hermione, Imogen, Prospero, — these are, as it were, names for the gracious powers which extend forgiveness to men. From the first, Hermione, whose clear-sightedness is equal to her courage, had perceived that her husband laboured under a delusion which was cruel and calamitous to himself. From the first, she transcends all blind resentment, and has true pity for the man who wrongs her. But, if she has fortitude for her own uses, she is also able to accept for her husband the inevitable pain which is needful to restore him to his better mind. She will not shorten the term of his suffering, because that suffering is beneficent. And at the last her silent embrace carries with it — and justly — a portion of that truth she had uttered long before : —

How will this grieve you,
When you shall come to clearer knowledge, that
You thus have publish'd me! Gentle my lord,
You scarce can right me throughly then, to say
You did mistake.

The calm and complete comprehension of the fact is a possession painful yet precious to Hermione ; and it lifts her
above all vulgar confusion of heart or temper, and above all
unjust resentment.

Imogen, who is the reverse of grave and massive in character, but who has an exquisite vivacity of feeling and fancy,
and a heart pure, quick, and ardent, passes from the swoon
of her sudden anguish to a mood of bright and keen resentment, which is free from every trace of vindictive passion,
and is indeed only pain disguised. And in like manner she
forgives, not with self-possession and a broad, tranquil joy in
the accomplished fact, but through a pure ardour, an exquisite eagerness of love and delight. Prospero's forgiveness is
solemn, judicial, and has in it something abstract and imper-
sonal. He cannot wrong his own higher nature, he cannot
wrong his nobler reason, by cherishing so unworthy a passion
as the desire of vengeance. Sebastian and Antonio, from whose
conscience no remorse has been elicited, are met by no comfortable pardon. They have received their lesson of failure
and pain, and may possibly be convinced of the good sense
and prudence of honourable dealing, even if they cannot perceive its moral obligation. Alonso, who is repentant, is sol-
emnly pardoned. The forgiveness of Prospero is an embod-
iment of impartial wisdom and loving justice.

When a man has attained some high and luminous table-
land of joy or of renouncement ; when he has really trans-
cended self; or when some one of the everlasting virtuous
powers of the world, — duty, or sacrifice, or the strength of

any thing higher than oneself, — has assumed authority over him ; forthwith a strange, pathetic, ideal light is shed over all beautiful things in the lower world which has been abandoned.   We see the sunlight on our neighbour's field, while we are preoccupied about the grain that is growing in our own.   And when we have ceased to hug our souls to any material possession, we see the sunlight wherever it falls.   In the last chapter of George Eliot's great novel, Romola, who has ascended into *her* clear and calm solitude of self-transcending duty, bends tenderly over the children of Tito, uttering, in words made simple for their needs, the lore she has learnt from life, and seeing on their faces the light of strange, ideal beauty.   In the latest plays of Shakespeare, the sympathetic reader can discern unmistakably a certain abandonment of the common joy of the world, a certain remoteness from the usual pleasures and sadnesses of life, and at the same time, all the more, this tender bending over those who are like children, still absorbed in their individual joys and sorrows.

Over the beauty of youth and the love of youth there is shed, in these plays of Shakespeare's final period, a clear yet tender luminousness, not elsewhere to be perceived in his writings.   In his earlier plays, Shakespeare writes concerning young men and maidens, their loves, their mirth, their griefs, as one who is among them, who has a lively personal interest in their concerns, who can make merry with them, treat them familiarly, and, if need be, can mock them into good sense. There is nothing in these early plays wonderful, strangely beautiful, pathetic about youth and its joys and sorrows.   In the histories and tragedies, as was to be expected, mor⸱ ⸱ sive, broader, or more profound objects of interes the Poet's attention.   But, in these latest plays, † ful pathetic light is always present. There are the sufferers, aged, experienced, tried, — Queen Catharine, Prospero, Hermione. And over against these there are the children absorbed in their happy and exquisite egoism, — Perdita and Miranda, Florizel and Ferdinand, and the boys of old Belarius.

The same means to secure ideality for these figures, so young and beautiful, is in each case (instinctively, perhaps, rather than deliberately) resorted to. They are lost children, — princes or princesses, removed from the Court, and its conventional surroundings, into some scene of rare natural beauty. There are the lost princes, Arviragus and Guiderius, among the mountains of Wales, drinking the free air, and offering their salutations to the risen Sun. There is Perdita, the shepherdess-princess, "queen of curds and cream," sharing with old and young her flowers, lovelier and more undying than those that Proserpina let fall from Dis's wagon. There is Miranda, (whose very name is significant of wonder,) made up of beauty, and love, and womanly pity, neither courtly nor rustic, with the breeding of an island of enchantment, where Prospero is her tutor and protector, and Caliban her servant, and the Prince of Naples her lover. In each of these plays we can see Shakespeare, as it were, tenderly bending over the joys and sorrows of youth. We recognize this rather through the total characterization, and through a feeling and a presence, than through definite incident or statement. But some of this feeling escapes in the disinterested joy and admiration of old Belarius when he sees the princely youths, and in Camillo's loyalty to Florizel; while it obtains more distinct expression in the words which Prospero utters, when from a distance he sees Miranda's zeal to relieve

Ferdinand from his task of log-bearing : " Poor worm, thou art infected."

It is not chiefly because Prospero is a great enchanter, now about to break his magic staff, to drown his book deeper than ever plummet sounded, to dismiss his airy spirits, and to return to the practical service of his Dukedom, that we identify him in some measure with Shakespeare himself. It is rather because the temper of Prospero, the grave harmony of his character, his self-mastery, his calm validity of will, his sensitiveness to wrong, his unfaltering justice, and, with these, a certain abandonment, a remoteness from the common joys and sorrows of the world, are characteristic of Shakespeare as discovered to us in all his latest plays. Prospero is a harmonious and fully-developed *will.* In the earlier play of fairy enchantments, *A Midsummer-Night's Dream*, the " human mortals " wander to and fro in a maze of error, misled by the mischievous frolic of Puck, the jester and clown of Fairyland. But here the spirits of the elements, and Caliban the gross genius of brute-matter, — needful for the service of life, — are brought under subjection to the human will of Prospero.

What is more, Prospero has entered into complete possession of himself. Shakespeare has shown us his quick sense of injury, his intellectual impatience, his occasional moment of keen irritability, in order that we may be more deeply aware of his abiding strength and self-possession, and that we may perceive how these have been grafted upon a temperament not impassive or unexcitable. And Prospero has reached not only the higher levels of moral attainment ; he has also reached an altitude of thought from which he can survey the whole of human life, and see how small and yet how great it is. His heart is sensitive, he is profoundly.

touched by the joy of children, with whom in the egoism of
their love he passes for a thing of secondary interest; he is
deeply moved by the perfidy of his brother. His brain is
readily set a-work, and can with difficulty be checked from
eager and excessive energizing; he is subject to the access
of sudden and agitating thought. But Prospero masters his
own sensitiveness, emotional and intellectual: —

> We are such stuff
> As dreams are made on, and our little life
> Is rounded with a sleep. Sir, I am vex'd;
> Bear with my weakness; my old brain is troubled:
> Be not disturb'd with my infirmity:
> If you be pleased, retire into my cell,
> And there repose: a turn or two I'll walk,
> To still my beating mind.

"Such stuff as dreams are made on." Nevertheless, in
this little life, in this dream, Prospero will maintain his dream-
rights and fulfil his dream-duties. In the dream, he, a Duke,
will accomplish Duke's work. Having idealized every thing,
Shakespeare left every thing real. Bishop Berkeley's foot
was no less able to set a pebble flying than was the lumber-
ing foot of Dr. Johnson. Nevertheless, no material substance
intervened between the soul of Berkeley and the immediate
presence of the play of Divine power.

A thought which seems to run through the whole of *The
Tempest*, appearing here and there like a coloured thread in
some web, is the thought that the true freedom of man consists in service. Ariel, untouched by human feeling, is pant-
ing for his liberty: in the last words of Prospero are promised his enfranchisement and dismissal to the elements. Ariel
reverences his great master, and serves him with bright
alacrity; but he is bound by none of our human ties, strong
and tender; and he will rejoice when Prospero is to him as

though he never were. To Caliban, a land-fish, with the
duller elements of earth and water in his composition, but
no portion of the higher elements, air and fire, though he
receives dim intimations of a higher world, — a musical humming, or a twangling, or a voice heard in sleep ; — to Caliban, service is slavery. He hates to bear his logs ; he fears
the incomprehensible power of Prospero, and obeys, and
curses. The great master has usurped the rights of the
brute-power Caliban. And when Stephano and Trinculo
appear, ridiculously impoverished specimens of humanity,
with their shallow understandings and vulgar greeds, this
poor earth-monster is possessed by a sudden fanaticism for
liberty ! —

> 'Ban, 'Ban, Ca—Caliban
> Has a new master: get a new man.
> Freedom, hey-day! hey-day, freedom! freedom, hey-day, freedom!

His new master also sings his impassioned hymn of liberty, the *Marseillaise* of the enchanted island : —

> Flout 'em and scout 'em, and scout 'em and flout 'em ;
> Thought is free.

The leaders of the revolution, escaped from the stench
and foulness of the horse-pond, King Stephano and his
prime minister Trinculo, like too many leaders of the people,
bring to an end their great achievement on behalf of liberty
by quarrelling over booty, — the trumpery which the providence of Prospero had placed in their way. Caliban, though
scarce more truly wise or instructed than before, at least discovers his particular error of the day and hour : —

> What a thrice-double ass
> Was I, to take this drunkard for a god,
> And worship this dull fool !

It must be admitted that Shakespeare, if not, as Hav Coleridge asserted, "a Tory and a gentleman," had within him some of the elements of English conservatism.

But, while Ariel and Caliban, each in his own way, are impatient of service, the human actors, in whom we are chiefly interested, are entering into bonds, — bonds of affection, bonds of duty, in which they find their truest freedom. Ferdinand and Miranda emulously contend in the task of bearing the burden which Prospero has imposed upon the Prince : —

> I am, in my condition,
> A prince, Miranda; I do think, a king, —
> I would, not so! — and would no more endure
> This wooden slavery than to suffer
> The flesh-fly blow my mouth.   Hear my soul speak:
> The very instant that I saw you, did
> My heart fly to your service; there resides,
> To make me slave to it; and for your sake
> Am I this patient log-man.

And Miranda speaks with the sacred candour from which spring the nobler manners of a world more real and glad than the world of convention and proprieties and pruderies : —

> Hence, bashful cunning!
> And prompt me, plain and holy innocence!
> I am your wife, if you will marry me;
> If not, I'll die your maid: to be your fellow
> You may deny me; but I'll be your servant,
> Whether you will or no.
>   *Ferd.*   My mistress, dearest,
> And I thus humble ever.
>   *Mira.*   My husband, then?
>   *Ferd.* Ay, with a heart as willing
> As bondage e'er of freedom.

In an earlier part of the play, this chord which runs through it had been playfully struck in the description of

Gzalo's imaginary commonwealth, in which man is to be
enfranchised from all the laborious necessities of life. Here
is the ideal notional liberty, Shakespeare would say ; and to
attempt to realize it at once lands us in absurdities and self-
contradictions : —

> For no kind of traffic
> Would I admit; no name of magistrate;
> Letters should not be known; riches, poverty,
> And use of service, none; contract, succession,
> Bourn, bound of land, tilth, vineyard, none;
> No use of metal, corn, or wine, or oil;
> No occupation; all men idle, all,
> And women too, but innocent and pure;
> No sovereignty : —
>   *Sebas.*   Yet he would be king on't.
>   *Anto.* The latter end of his commonwealth forgets the beginning.

THE TEMPEST.

PERSONS REPRESENTED.

ALONSO, King of Naples.
SEBASTIAN, his Brother.
PROSPERO, the rightful Duke of Milan.
ANTONIO, his Brother, the usurping Duke of Milan.
FERDINAND, Son to the King of Naples.
GONZALO, an honest old Counsellor of Naples.
ADRIAN, } Lords.
FRANCISCO, }
CALIBAN, a savage and deformed Slave.

TRINCULO, a Jester.
STEPHANO, a drunken Butler.
Master of a Ship, Boatswain, and Mariners.

MIRANDA, Daughter to Prospero.

ARIEL, an airy Spirit.
Other Spirits attending on Prospero.
IRIS,
CERES,
JUNO, } presented by Spirits.
Nymphs,
Reapers,

SCENE, *a Ship at Sea; afterwards an uninhabited Island.*

ACT I.

SCENE I. — *On a Ship at sea.   A Storm, with Thunder and Lightning.*

Enter Master *and* Boatswain *severally.*

Mast. Boatswain !
Boats. Here, master : what cheer?

43

Mast. Good,[1] speak to the mariners : fall to't yarely,[2] or we run ourselves a-ground : bestir, bestir.   [*Exit.*

Enter Mariners.

Boats. Heigh, my hearts ! cheerly, cheerly, my hearts ! yare, yare ! Take in the topsail. Tend to the master's whistle. [*Exeunt* Mariners.] — Blow till thou burst thy wind,[3] if room enough ![4]

Enter ALONSO, SEBASTIAN, ANTONIO, FERDINAND, GONZALO, *and Others.*

Alon. Good boatswain, have care. Where's the master? Play the men.[5]

Boats. I pray now, keep below.

Anto. Where is the master, boatswain?

Boats. Do you not hear him? You mar our labour: keep your cabins ; you do assist the storm.

---

[1] Here, as in many other places, *good* is used just as we now use *well.* So a little after: "*Good,* yet remember whom thou hast aboard." Also in *Hamlet,* i. 1: "*Good* now, sit down, and tell me," &c. In the text, however, it carries something of an evasive force; as, "Let that go"; or, "No matter for that."

[2] *Yarely* is *nimbly, briskly,* or *alertly.* So, in the next speech, *yare,* an imperative verb, is, *be nimble,* or *be on the alert.* The word is seldom if ever used now in any form, but was much used in the Poet's time. In North's Plutarch we have such phrases as "galleys not *yare* of steerage," and "ships light of *yarage,*" and "galleys heavy of *yarage.*"

[3] In Shakespeare's time, the wind was often represented pictorially by the figure of a man with his cheeks puffed out to their utmost tension with the act of blowing. Probably the Poet had such a figure in his mind. So in *King Lear,* iii. 2 : "Blow, winds, and *crack your cheeks !*" Also in *Pericles,* iii. 1 : "Blow, and split thyself."

[4] That is, "if *we have* sea-room enough." So in *Pericles,* iii. 1 : "But *sea-room,* an the brine and cloudy billow kiss the Moon, I care not."

[5] Act with spirit, behave like men. So in 2 Samuel, x. 12: "Be of good courage, and let us *play the men* for our people."

Gonza. Nay, good, be patient.

Boats. When the sea is. Hence! What care these roarers for the name of king? To cabin: silence! trouble us not.

Gonza. Good, yet remember whom thou hast aboard.

Boats. None that I more love than myself. You are a counsellor: if you can command these elements to silence, and work the peace of the present,[6] we will not hand a rope more; use your authority: if you cannot, give thanks you have lived so long, and make yourself ready in your cabin for the mischance of the hour, if it so hap. — Cheerly, good hearts! — Out of our way, I say.   [*Exit.*

Gonza. I have great comfort from this fellow: methinks he hath no drowning-mark upon him; his complexion[7] is perfect gallows. — Stand fast, good Fate, to his hanging! make the rope of his destiny our cable, for our own doth little advantage! If he be not born to be hang'd, our case is miserable.   [*Exeunt.*

Re-enter Boatswain.

Boats. Down with the top-mast![8] yare; lower, lower! Bring her to try wi' th' main-course.[9] [*A cry within.*] A

---

[6] *Present* for *present time.* So in the Prayer-Book: "That those things may please Him which we do at this *present.*" And in 1 Corinthians, xv. 6: "Of whom the greater part remain unto this *present.*"

[7] *Complexion* was often used for *nature, native bent* or *aptitude.* See *The Merchant of Venice,* page 134, note 7.

[8] Of this order Lord Mulgrave, a sailor critic, says, "The striking the top-mast was a new invention in Shakespeare's time, which he here very properly introduces. He has placed his ship in the situation in which it was indisputably right to strike the top-mast, — where he had not sea-room."

[9] This appears to have been a common nautical phrase. So in Hackluyt's *Voyages,* 1598: "And when the bark had way we cut the hauser, and so gat the sea to our friend, and *tried out* all the day *with our maine* course." Also in Smith's *Sea Grammar,* 1627: "Let us lie at *trie with our maine*

plague upon this howling ! they are louder than the weather
or our office.[10] —

Re-enter SEBASTIAN, ANTONIO, *and* GONZALO.

Yet again ! what do you here? Shall we give o'er, and
drown? Have you a mind to sink?

Sebas. A pox o' your throat, you bawling, blasphemous,
incharitable dog !

Boats. Work you, then.

Anto. Hang, cur, hang ! you whoreson, insolent noise-
maker, we are less afraid to be drown'd[11] than thou art.

Gonza. I'll warrant him for drowning,[12] though the ship
were no stronger than a nut-shell.

Boats. Lay her a-hold, a-hold ! set her two courses ![13] off
to sea again ; lay her off !

---

course." And Sir Walter Raleigh speaks of being "obliged to lye at trye
with our main course and mizen." *To lie at try* is to keep as close to the
wind as possible.

[10] *Weather* for *storm.* "Their howling drowns both the roaring of the
tempest and the commands of the officer," or "our official orders."

[11] "Less afraid *of being* drown'd." So the Poet often uses the infinitive
gerundively, or like the Latin *gerund.* See *King Lear*, page 117, note 18;
also page 205, note 28.

[12] *As to,* or *as regards,* drowning. A not uncommon use of *for.* — Gonzalo has in mind the old proverb, "He that is born to be hanged will never
be drowned."

[13] A ship's *courses* are her largest lower sails; "so called," says Holt,
"because they contribute most to give her way through the water, and thus
enable her to feel the helm, and steer her *course* better than when they are
not *set* or spread to the wind." Captain Glascock, another sailor critic,
comments thus: "The ship's head is to be put leeward, and the vessel to
be drawn off the land under that canvas nautically denominated the two
courses." To *lay a ship a-hold* is to bring her to lie as near the wind as
she can, in order to keep clear of the land, and get her out to sea. So Admiral Smith, in his *Sailors' Wordbook:* "A hold: A term of our early navi-
gators, for bringing a ship close to the wind, so as to hold or keep to it."

Re-enter Mariners, *wet.*

Mariners. All lost ! to prayers, to prayers ! all lost !

[*Exeunt.*

Boats. What, must our mouths be cold ?

Gonza. The King and Prince at prayers ! let us assist
    them,

For our case is as theirs.

Sebas.   I'm out of patience.

Anto. We're merely [14] cheated out of our lives by drunk-
    ards.

This wide-chopp'd rascal — would thou mightst lie drown-
    ing,

The washing of ten tides !

Gonza.   He'll be hang'd yet,

Though every drop of water swear against it,

And gape at widest to glut him. [15]

A confused noise within. Mercy on us ! We split, we
split ! — Farewell, my wife and children ! — Farewell, brother ! — We split, we split, we split !   [*Exit* Boatswain.

Anto. Let's all sink wi' th' King. [16]   [*Exit.*

Sebas. Let's take leave of him.   [*Exit.*

Gonza. Now would I give a thousand furlongs of sea for
an acre of barren ground ; ling, heath, broom, furze, any

---

[14] *Merely*, here, is *utterly* or *absolutely.* A frequent usage. So in *Hamlet*,
i. 2 : "Things rank and gross in nature possess it *merely.*"

[15] *Glut* for *englut;* that is, *swallow up.* — *Widest* is here a monosyllable.
The same with many words that are commonly two syllables.

[16] This double elision of *with* and *the*, so as to draw the two into one
syllable, is quite frequent, especially in the Poet's later plays. So before in
this scene : " Bring her to try *wi' th'* main course." Single elisions for the
same purpose, such as *by th'*, *for th'*, *from th'*, *to th'*, &c., are still more frequent. So in the first speech of the next scene : " Mounting *to th'* welkin's
cheek."

thing.[17] The wills above [18] be done ! but I would fain die a
dry death.[19]   [*Exit.*

SCENE II. — *The Island: before the Cell of* PROSPERO.

Enter PROSPERO *and* MIRANDA.

Mira. If by your art, my dearest father, you have
Put the wild waters in this roar, allay them.
The sky, it seems, would pour down stinking pitch,
But that the sea, mounting to th' welkin's cheek,[1]
Dashes the fire out.   O, I have suffer'd
With those that I saw suffer ! a brave [2] vessel,
Who had no doubt some noble creatures in her,

---

[17] *Ling, heath, broom,* and *furze* were names of plants growing on British
barrens. So in Harrison's description of Britain, prefixed to Holinshed:
"*Brome, heth, firze,* brakes, whinnes, *ling,* &c."

[18] Of course, "the *wills* above " is the *will* of the *Powers* above.

[19] The first scene of *The Tempest* is a very striking instance of the great
accuracy of Shakespeare's knowledge in a professional science, the most
difficult to attain without the help of experience. He must have acquired
it by conversation with some of the most skilful seamen of that time. The
succession of events is strictly observed in the natural progress of the distress described ; the expedients adopted are the most proper that could
have been devised for a chance of safety : and it is neither to the want of
skill of the seamen or the bad qualities of the ship, but solely to the power
of Prospero, that the shipwreck is to be attributed. The words of command
are not only strictly proper, but are only such as point the object to be attained,
and no superfluous ones of detail. Shakespeare's ship was too well manned
to make it necessary to tell the seamen how they were to do it, as well as
what they were to do. — LORD MULGRAVE.

[1] *Welkin* is *sky.* We have other like expressions ; as, "the cloudy cheeks
of heaven," in *Richard the Second,* and "the wide cheeks o' the air," in
Coriolanus. — The hyperbole of waves rolling sky-high occurs repeatedly.
So in *The Winter's Tale,* iii. 3 : " Now the ship boring the Moon with her
main-mast, and anon swallowed with yeast and froth." And in *Othello,* ii. 1 :
" The wind-shaked surge seems to cast water on the burning bear."

[2] *Brave* is *fine* or *splendid ;* like the Scottish *braw.* Repeatedly so in this
play, as also elsewhere.

Dash'd all to pieces.   O, the cry did knock
Against my very heart !   Poor souls, they perish'd !
Had I been any god of power, I would
Have sunk the sea within the earth, or e'er [3]
It should the good ship so have swallow'd, and
The fraughting souls [4] within her.

    Pros.   Be collected ;
No more amazement : [5] tell your piteous heart
There's no harm done.

    Mira.   O, woe the day !

    Pros.   No harm.
I have done nothing but in care of thee, —
Of thee, my dear one, thee, my daughter, — who
Art ignorant of what thou art, nought knowing
Of whence I am ; nor that I am more better [6]
Than Prospero, master of a full-poor cell,
And thy no greater father.

    Mira.   More to know
Did never meddle [7] with my thoughts.

    Pros.   'Tis time
I should inform thee further.   Lend thy hand,
And pluck my magic garment from me. — So :

                             [Lays down his robe.

---

[3] *Or e'er* is *before* or *sooner than.*   So in Ecclesiastes, xii. 6: "*Or ever* the silver cord be loosed."   See, also, *Hamlet*, page 62, note 31.

[4] *Fraught* is an old form of *freight.*   Present usage would require *fraughted.* In Shakespeare's time, the active and passive forms were very often used indiscriminately.   So, here, "fraughting souls" is *freighted* souls, or souls on freight.

[5] The sense of *amazement* was much stronger than it is now.   Here it is *anguish* or *distress* of mind.

[6] This doubling of comparatives occurs continually in all the writers of Shakespeare's time.   The same with superlatives.

[7] To *meddle* is, properly, to *mix,* to *mingle.*

Lie there, my art.[8] —Wipe thou thine eyes ; have comfort.
The direful spectacle of the wreck, which touch'd
The very virtue of compassion in thee,
I have with such prevision in mine art
So safely order'd, that there is no soul[9]—
No, not so much perdition as an hair
Betid to any creature in the vessel
Which thou heard'st cry, which thou saw'st sink.   Sit down ;
For thou must now know further.
          Mira.   You have often
Begun to tell me what I am ; but stopp'd,
And left me to a bootless inquisition,
Concluding, *Stay, not yet.*
          Pros.   The hour's now come ;
The very minute bids thee ope thine ear :
Obey, and be attentive.   Canst thou remember
A time before we came unto this cell?
I do not think thou canst ; for then thou wast not
Out three years old.[10]
          Mira.   Certainly, sir, I can.
          Pros. By what? by any other house or person?
Of any thing the image tell me that
Hath kept with thy remembrance.
          Mira.   - 'Tis far off,
And rather like a dream than an assurance
That my remembrance warrants.   Had I not

    [8] Lord Burleigh, at night when he put off his gown, used to say, " Lie
there, Lord Treasurer"; and, bidding adieu to all State affairs, disposed
himself to his quiet rest.—FULLER'S *Holy State.*
    [9] The sense is here left incomplete, and purposely, no doubt.   Prospero
has many like changes of construction in this part of the scene.
    [10] Not *fully* three-years old.   We have a like use of *out* in iv. 1 : " But
play with sparrows, and be a boy right *out.*"

Four or five women once that tended me?

Pros. Thou hadst, and more, Miranda.   But how is it
That this lives in thy mind?   What see'st thou else
In the dark backward and abysm [11] of time?
If thou remember'st aught ere thou camest here,
How thou camest here, thou mayst. [12]

    Mira.   But that I do not.

    Pros. Twelve year since, Miranda, twelve year [13] since,
Thy father was the Duke of Milan, and
A prince of power.

    Mira.   Sir, are you not my father?

    Pros. Thy mother was a piece of virtue, and
She said thou wast my daughter; and thy father
Was Duke of Milan; thou his only heir,
A princess, — no worse issued.

    Mira.   O the Heavens!
What foul play had we, that we came from thence?
Or blessèd was't we did?

    Pros.   Both, both, my girl:
By foul play, as thou say'st, were we heaved thence;
But blessedly holp [14] hither.

    Mira.   O, my heart bleeds
To think o' the teen [15] that I have turn'd you to,

---

[11] *Abysm* is an old form of *abyss;* from the old French *abisme.*

[12] "If thou remember'st aught *ere* thou camest here, thou mayst also remember *how* thou camest here."

[13] In words denoting time, space, and quantity, the singular form was often used with the plural sense. So we have *mile* and *pound* for *miles* and *pounds.* — In this line, the first *year* is two syllables, the second one. Often so with various other words, such as *hour, fire,* &c.

[14] *Holp* or *holpen* is the old preterite of *help;* occurring continually in *The Psalter,* which is an older translation of the Psalms than that in the Bible.

[15] *Teen* is an old word for *trouble, anxiety,* or *sorrow.* So in *Love's Labours Lost,* iv. 3: "Of sighs, of groans, of sorrow, and of *teen.*"

Which is from my remembrance !   Please you, further.

Pros. My brother, and thy uncle, call'd Antonio, —
I pray thee, mark me ; — that a brother should
· Be so perfidious ! — he whom, next thyself,
Of all the world I loved, and to him put
The manage [16] of my State ; as, at that time,
Through all the signiories it was the first,[17]
And Prospero the prime Duke ; being so reputed
In dignity, and for the liberal arts
Without a parallel : those being all my study,
The government I cast upon my brother,
And to my State grew stranger, being transported
And rapt in secret studies.   Thy false uncle, —
Dost thou attend me?

Mira.   Sir, most heedfully.

Pros. — Being once perfected how to grant suits,
How to deny them ; who [18] t' advance, and who
To trash for over-topping,[19] — new-created
The creatures that were mine, I say, or changed 'em,·
Or else new-form'd 'em ; having both the key
Of officer and office,[20] set all hearts i' the State
To what tune pleased his ear ; that [21] now he was

[16] *Manage* for *management* or *administration*. Repeatedly so.

[17] *Signiory* for *lordship* or *principality*. Botero, in his *Relations of the World*, 1630, says, " Milan claims to be the first duchy in Europe."·

. [18] This use of *who* where present usage requires *whom* was not ungrammatical in Shakespeare's time.

[19] To *trash* for *overtopping* is to *check* the *overgrowth*, to reduce the exorbitancy. The word seems to have been a hunting-term for checking the speed of hounds when too forward ; the *trash* being a strap or rope fastened to the dog's neck, and dragging on the ground. The sense of *clogging* or *keeping back* is the right antithesis to *advance*.

[20] " The *key* of officer and office " is the *tuning* key ; as of a piano. ·

[21] *That* is here equivalent to *so that*, or *insomuch that*. Continually so in old poetry, and not seldom in old prose. ·

The ivy which had hid my princely trunk,
And suck'd the verdure out on't.   Thou attend'st not.[22]
   Mira. O good sir, I do.
   Pros.   I pray thee, mark me.
I thus neglecting worldly ends, all dedicated
To closeness, and the bettering of my mind
With that which, but[23] by being so retired,
O'er-prized all popular rate,[24] in my false brother
Awaked an evil nature ; and my trust,
Like a good parent, did beget of him
A falsehood, in its contrary as great
As my trust was ; which had indeed no limit,
A confidence sans[25] bound.   He being thus lorded,
Not only with what my revénue[26] yielded,
But what my power might else exact, — like one
Who having unto truth, by falsing of it,[27]

[22] The old gentleman thinks his daughter is not attending to his tale, because his own thoughts keep wandering from it ; his mind being filled with other things, — the tempest he has got up, and the consequences of it. This absence or distraction of mind aptly registers itself in the irregular and broken style of his narrative.

[23] This is the exceptive *but*, as it is called, and has the force of *be out*, of which it is, indeed, an old contraction. So later in this scene : "And, *but* he's something stain'd with grief," &c.; where *but* evidently has the force of *except that*.

[24] The meaning seems to be, "Which would have exceeded all popular estimate, but that it withdrew me from my public duties"; as if he were sensible of his error in getting so "rapt in secret studies" as to leave the State a prey to violence and usurpation.

[25] *Sans* is the French equivalent for *without*. The Poet uses it whenever he wants a monosyllable with that meaning.

[26] Shakespeare, in a few instances, has *revenue* with the accent on the first syllable, as in the vulgar pronunciation of our time. Here the accent is on the second syllable, as it should be. See *Hamlet*, page 135, note 8.

[27] The verb to *false* was often used for to *treat falsely*, to *falsify*, to *forge*, to *lie*. So in *Cymbeline*, ii. 3: "And make Diana's rangers *false* them-

Made such a sinner of his memory
To credit [28] his own lie, — he did believe
He was indeed the Duke; out o' the substitution, [29]
And executing the outward face of royalty,
With all prerogative : hence his ambition growing, —
Dost thou hear? [30]

   Mira.   Your tale, sir, would cure deafness.

   Pros. To have no screen between this part he play'd
And them he play'd it for, [31] he needs will be
Absolute Milan.   Me, [32] poor man, my library
Was dukedom large enough : of temporal royalties
He thinks me now incapable ; confederates —
So dry he was for sway [33] — wi' th' King of Naples
To give him annual tribute, do him homage,
Subject his coronet to his crown, and bend
The dukedom, yet unbow'd, — alas, poor Milan ! —
To most ignoble stooping.

selves." And in *The Faerie Queene*, ii. 1, 1: "Whom Princes late displeasure left in bands, for *falsèd* letters." Also in i. 3, 30: "And in his *falsèd*
fancy he her takes to be the fairest wight," &c. And in Drant's Horace:
"The taverner that *falseth* othes, and little reckes to lye."—The pronoun
it may refer to *truth*, or may be used absolutely; probably the former. The
Poet has such phrases as to *prince it*, for to *act the prince*, and to *monster it*
for to *be a monster*. And so the word is often used now in all sorts of speech
and writing; as to *brase it out*, and to *foot it through*. See Critical Notes.

  [28] "*As* to credit" is the meaning. The Poet often omits *as* in such
cases. Sometimes he omits both of the correlatives *so* and *as*.

  [29] That is, "*in consequence* of his being my substitute or deputy."

  [30] In this place, *hear* was probably meant as a dissyllable; just as *year* a
little before. So, at all events, the verse requires.

  [31] This is well explained by Mr. P. A. Daniel: "Prospero was the screen
behind which the traitorous Antonio governed the people of Milan; and, to
remove this screen between himself and them, he conspired his brother's
overthrow."

  [32] "*For* me" is the meaning. Such ellipses are frequent.

  [33] So *thirsty* for power or rule; no uncommon use of *dry* now.

Mira.   O the Heavens !

Pros. Mark his condition, and th' event ;[34] then tell me,
If this might be a brother.

Mira.   I should sin
To think but nobly [35] of my grandmother.

Pros. Good wombs have borne bad sons.   Now the con-
    dition :
This King of Naples, being an enemy
To me inveterate, hearkens my brother's suit ;
Which was, that he, in lieu o' the premises,[36] —
Of homage, and I know not how much tribute, —
Should presently [37] extirpate me and mine
Out of the dukedom, and confer fair Milan,
With all the honours, on my brother : whereon,
A treacherous army levied, one midnight
Fated to th' practice [38] did Antonio open
The gates of Milan ; and, i' the dead of darkness,
The ministers for th' purpose hurried thence
Me and thy crying self.

Mira.   Alack, for pity !
I, not remembering how I cried on't then,
Will cry it o'er again : it is a hint [39]
That wrings mine eyes to't.

Pros.   Hear a little further,

---

[34] *Condition* is the terms of his compact with the King of Naples ;· *event,*
the consequences that followed.

[35] "*But* nobly " is *otherwise than* nobly, of course.

[36] *In lieu of* is *in return for,* or *in consideration of.* Shakespeare never
uses the phrase in its present meaning, *instead of.*

[37] *Presently* is *immediately* or *forthwith.* A frequent usage.

[38] *Plot, stratagem, contrivance* are old meanings of *practice.*

[39] *Hint* for *cause* or *theme.* A frequent usage. So again in ii. 1: "Our
hint of woe is common."

And then I'll bring thee to the present business
Which now's upon's; without the which this story
Were most impertinent.[40]

   Mira.   Wherefore did they not
That hour destroy us?

   Pros.   Well demanded, wench : [41]
My tale provokes that question.   Dear, they durst not —
So dear the love my people bore me — set
A mark so bloody on the business; but
With colours fairer painted their foul ends.
In few,[42] they hurried us aboard a bark,
Bore us some leagues to sea; where they prepared
A rotten carcass of a boat, not rigg'd,
Nor tackle, sail, nor mast; the very rats
Instinctively had quit it: there they hoist us,[43]
To cry to th' sea that roar'd to us; to sigh
To th' winds, whose pity, sighing back again,
Did us but loving wrong.

   Mira.   .   Alack, what trouble
Was I then to you !

   Pros.   O, a cherubin
Thou wast that did preserve me !   Thou didst smile,
Infusèd with a fortitude from Heaven,
When I have degg'd[44] the sea with drops full salt,

---

   [40] *Impertinent* is *irrelevant*, or *out of place; not pertinent;* the old meaning of the word.   The Poet never uses *irrelevant.*

   [41] *Wench* was a common term of affectionate familiarity.

   [42] That is, in few *words*, in *short*.   Often so.

   [43] *Hoist* for *hoisted;* as, a little before, *quit* for *quitted.*   So in *Hamlet*,
iii. 4: " 'Tis the sport to have the engineer *hoist* with his own petar."   The
Poet has many preterites so formed.   And the same usage occurs in *The
Psalter;* as in the 93d Psalm: "The floods are risen, O Lord, the floods
have *lift* up their voice."

   [44] To *deg* is an old provincial word for to *sprinkle.*   So explained in

Under my burden groan'd; which raised in me
An undergoing stomach,[45] to bear up
Against what should ensue.
  Mira.   How came we ashore?
  Pros. By Providence divine.
Some food we had, and some fresh water, that
A noble Neapolitan, Gonzalo,
Out of his charity, — being then appointed
Master of this design, — did give us; with
Rich garments, linens, stuffs, and necessaries,
Which since have steaded much;[46] so, of his gentleness,
Knowing I loved my books, he furnish'd me,
From mine own library, with volumes that
I prize above my dukedom.
  Mira.   Would I might
But ever see that man!
  Pros.   Now I arise:[47]

Carr's *Glossary:* "To *deg* clothes is to sprinkle them with water previous to ironing." And in Atkinson's *Glossary of the Cleveland Dialect, degg* or *dagg* is explained "to sprinkle with water, to drizzle." Also, in Brockett's *Glossary of North-Country Words:* "*Dag,* a drizzling rain, dew upon the grass."—The foregoing quotations are from the Clarendon edition. See Critical Notes.

[45] An *undergoing stomach* is an *enduring courage.* Shakespeare uses *stomach* repeatedly for *courage.*

[46] Have stood us in good stead, or done us much service.

[47] These words have been a great puzzle to the editors, and various explanations of them have been given. Staunton prints them as addressed to Ariel, and thinks this removes the difficulty. So taken, the words are meant to give Ariel notice that the speaker is now ready for his services in charming Miranda to sleep. But this does not seem to me very likely, as it makes Prospero give Ariel a second notice, in his next speech. So I rather adopt the explanation of Mr. William Aldis Wright, who thinks Prospero means that "the crisis in his own fortunes has come"; that he is now about to emerge from the troubles of which he has been speaking; and that he re-

Sit still, and hear the last of our sea-sorrow.
Here in this island we arrived ; and here
Have I, thy schoolmaster, made thee more profit [48]
Than other princesses can, that have more time
For vainer hours, and tutors not so careful.

   Mira. Heavens thank you for't ! And now, I pray you,
      sir, —
For still 'tis beating in my mind, — your reason
For raising this sea-storm?

   Pros.   Know thus far forth :
By accident most strange, bountiful Fortune —
Now my dear lady — hath mine enemies
Brought to this shore ; and by my prescience
I find my zenith [49] doth depend upon
A most auspicious star, whose influence
If now I court not, but omit, my fortunes
Will ever after droop.   Here cease more questions :
Thou art inclined to sleep ; 'tis a good dulness,
And give it way : I know thou canst not choose.[50] —

                      [MIRANDA *sleeps.*

gards this "reappearance from obscurity as a kind of resurrection, like the
rising of the Sun." This view is fully approved by Mr. Joseph Crosby.

  [48] *Profit* is here a verb : " Have *caused* thee to profit more," &c.

  [49] The common explanation of this is, " In astrological language *zenith*
is the *highest point* in one's fortunes." But I much prefer Mr. Crosby's explanation, who writes me as follows : " Note, here, the blending of ideas by
the speaker : he means to say, ' My fortune depends upon a star which,
being now in its zenith, is auspicious to me.' "

  [50] In the second scene, Prospero's speeches, till the entrance of Ariel,
contain the finest example I remember of retrospective narration for the
purpose of exciting immediate interest, and putting the audience in possession of all the information necessary for the understanding of the plot. Observe, too, the perfect probability of the moment chosen by Prospero to open
out the truth to his daughter, his own romantic bearing, and how completely any thing that might have been disagreeable to us in the magician·

Come away, servant, come ! I'm ready now :
Approach, my Ariel ; come !

Enter ARIEL.

Ari. All hail, great master ! grave sir, hail ! I come
To answer thy best pleasure ; be't to fly,
To swim, to dive into the fire, to ride
On the curl'd clouds : to thy strong bidding task
Ariel and all his quality.[51]
  Pros.   Hast thou, spirit,
Perform'd to point [52] the tempest that I bade thee ?
  Ari. To every article.
I boarded the King's ship ; now on the beak,
Now in the waist,[53] the deck, in every cabin,
I flamed amazement : sometime I'd divide,
And burn in many places ; on the top-mast,
The yards, and bowsprit, would I flame distinctly,[54]
Then meet and join. Jove's lightnings, the precursors
O'. the dreadful thunder-claps, more momentary [55]
And sight-outrunning were not : the fire, and cracks
Of sulphurous roaring, the most mighty Neptune

is reconciled and shaded in the humanity and natural feelings of the father.
In the very first speech of Miranda the simplicity and tenderness of her
character are at once laid open ; it would have been lost in direct contact
with the agitation of the first scene. — COLERIDGE.

 [51] That is, all of his *kind*, all his *fellow-spirits*, or who are like him.

 [52] Perform'd *exactly*, or in *every point* ; from the French *à point*.

 [53] *Beak*, the prow of the ship ; *waist*, the part between the quarter-deck
and forecastle.

 [54] So in the account of Robert Tomson's voyage, 1555, quoted by Mr.
Hunter : "This light continued aboard our ship about three hours, flying
from mast to mast, and from top to top ; and sometimes it would be in two
or three places at once." In the text, *distinctly* has the sense of *separately* ;
flaming in different places at the same time.

 [55] *Momentary* in the sense of *instantaneous.*

Seem'd to besiege, and make his bold waves tremble,
Yea, his dread trident shake.

    Pros.   My brave spirit !
Who was so firm, so constant, that this coil [56]
Would not infect his reason?

    Ari.   Not a soul
But felt a fever of the mad,[57] and play'd
Some tricks of desperation.   All but mariners
Plunged in the foaming brine, and quit the vessel,
Then all a-fire with me : the King's son, Ferdinand,
With hair up-staring,[58] — then like reeds, not hair, —
Was the first man that leap'd ; cried, *Hell is empty,*
And all the devils are here.

    Pros.   Why, that's my spirit !
But was not this nigh shore?

    Ari.   ·   Close by, my master.

    Pros. But are they, Ariel, safe?

    Ari.   Not a hair perish'd ;
On their unstaining [59] garments not a blemish,
But fresher than before : and, as thou badest me,
In troops I have dispersed them 'bout the isle.
The King's son have I landed by himself ;

---

[56] *Coil* is *stir, tumult,* or *disturbance.*

[57] Such a fever as madmen feel when the frantic fit is on them.

[58] *Upstaring* is *sticking out* "like quills upon the fretful porpentine." So in *The Faerie Queene,* vi. **11, 27** : " With ragged weedes, and *locks upstaring* hye." And in *Julius Cæsar,* iv. 3 : "Art thou some god, some angel, or some devil, that makest my blood cold, and my hair to *stare?*"

[59] *Unstaining* for *unstained;* another instance of the indiscriminate use of active and passive forms. This usage, both in participles and adjectives, is frequent all through these plays. So, in *The Winter's Tale,* iv. 4, we have " *discontenting* father" for *discontented* father; and in *Antony and Cleopatra,* iii. 13, " all-*obeying* breath" for all-*obeyed* breath, that is, breath that *all obey.* See, also, page 49, note 4.

Whom I left cooling of the air with sighs
In an odd angle [60] of the isle, and sitting,
His arms in this sad knot.[61]

    Pros.   Of the King's ship
The mariners, say, how hast thou disposed,
And all the rest o' the fleet?

    Ari.   Safely in harbour
Is the King's ship ; in the deep nook, where once
Thou call'dst me up at midnight to fetch dew
From the still-vex'd Bermoothes,[62] there she's hid :
The mariners all under hatches stow'd ;
Who, with a charm join'd to their suffer'd labour,
I've left asleep : and, for the rest o' the fleet
Which I dispersed, they all have met again,
And are upon the Mediterranean flote,[63]
Bound sadly home for Naples ;
Supposing that they saw the King's ship wreck'd,
And his great person perish.

    Pros.   Ariel, thy charge
Exactly is perform'd : but there's more work.

---

[60] *Odd angle* is *insignificant* or *out-of-the-way corner.*

[61] His arms folded up as in sorrowful meditation.

[62] *Still-vex'd* is *ever-troubled.* The Poet very often uses *still* in the sense of *ever* or *continually.* The Bermudas were supposed to be inhabited or haunted by witches and devils, and the sea around them to be agitated with perpetual storms. *Bermoothes* was then the common spelling of *Bermudas.* So in Fletcher's *Women Pleased,* i. 2: "The Devil should think of purchasing that egg-shell, to victual such a witch for the Burmoothes." Also in Webster's *Duchess of Malfi,* iii. 2: "I would sooner swim to the Bermootha's on two politicians' rotten bladders."

[63] *Flote,* like the French *flot,* is *flood, wave,* or *sea.* This passage shows that the scene of the play is *not* laid in the Bermudas, as there has not been time for the rest of the fleet to sail so far. And Ariel's trip to fetch the dew mentioned above was a much greater feat than going from one part of the Bermoothes to another.

What is the time o' the day?

Ari.   Past the mid season,
At least two glasses.[64]

Pros.   The time 'twixt six and now
Must by us both be spent most preciously.

Ari. Is there more toil? Since thou dost give me pains,
Let me remember [65] thee what thou hast promised,
Which is not yet perform'd me.

Pros.   How now! moody?
What is't thou canst demand?

Ari.   My liberty.

Pros. Before the time be out? no more!

Ari.   I pr'ythee,
Remember I have done thee worthy service ;
Told thee no lies, made no mistakings, served
Without or grudge or grumblings : thou didst promise
To bate me a full year.

Pros.   Dost thou forget
From what a torment I did free thee?

Ari.   No.

Pros. Thou dost ; and think'st it much to tread the ooze
Of the salt deep ; to run upon the sharp
Wind of the North ; to do me business in
The veins o' the earth when it is baked with frost.

Ari. I do not, sir.

Pros. Thou liest, malignant thing ![66]   Hast thou forgot
The foul witch Sycorax, who with age and envy [67]

---

[64] *Two glasses* is *two runnings* of the hour-glass.

[65] *Remember* for *remind*, or *put in mind.* Often so.

[66] Prospero should not be supposed to say this in earnest: he is merely
playing with his delicate and amiable minister.

[67] Here, as commonly in Shakespeare, *envy* is *malice.* And so he has
envious repeatedly for *malicious.* The usage was common.

Was grown into a hoop? hast thou forgot her?

 Ari. No, sir.

 Pros.   Thou hast : where was she born? speak ;
  tell me.

 Ari. Sir, in Argier.[68]

 Pros.   O, was she so? I must
Once in a month recount what thou hast been,
Which thou forgett'st. This damn'd witch Sycorax,
For mischiefs manifold, and sorceries terrible
To enter human hearing, from Argier,
Thou know'st, was banish'd : for one thing she had,[69]
They would not take her life. Is not this true?

 Ari. Ay, sir.

 Pros. This blue-eyed hag[70] was hither brought,
And here was left by th' sailors. Thou, my slave,
As thou report'st thyself, wast then her servant ;
And, for[71] thou wast a spirit too delicate
To act her earthy and abhorr'd commands,
Refusing her grand hests,[72] she did confine thee,
By help of her more potent ministers,
And in her most unmitigable rage,
Into a cloven pine ;[73] within which rift

---

 [68] *Argier* is the old English name for *Algiers.*

 [69] What this one thing was, appears in Prospero's next speech.

 [70] *Blue-eyed* and *blue eyes* were used, not for what we so designate, but for *blueness about the eyes.* So, in *As You Like It*, iii. 2, we have "a *blue eye*, and a sunken," to denote a gaunt, haggard, and cadaverous look." And so, in the text, *blue-eyed* is used as signifying extreme ugliness. In the Poet's time, what we call *blue* eyes were commonly called *gray*, and were considered eminently beautiful.

 [71] Here, as often, *for* is *because.* See *The Merchant*, page 96, note 6.

 [72] *Hests* is *commands, orders,* or *behests.*

 [73] *Into* and *in* were often used indiscriminately. Here, however, I suspect the sense of both words is implied : "She thrust you *into* a *splitted* pine, and there fastened you *in.*"

Imprison'd thou didst painfully remain
A dozen years; within which space she died,
And left thee there; where thou didst vent thy groans
As fast as mill-wheels strike.   Then was this island —
Save for the son that she did litter here,
A freckled whelp, hag-born — not honour'd with
A human shape.
    Ari.   Yes, Caliban her son.
    Pros. Dull thing, I say so; he, that Caliban,
Whom now I keep in service.   Thou best know'st
What torment I did find thee in: thy groans
Did make wolves howl, and penetrate the breasts
Of ever-angry bears.   It was a torment
To lay upon the damn'd, which Sycorax
Could not again undo: it was mine art,
When I arrived and heard thee, that made gape
The pine, and let thee out.
    Ari.   I thank thee, master.
    Pros. If thou more murmur'st, I will rend an oak,
And peg thee in his knotty entrails, till
Thou'st howl'd away twelve Winters.
    Ari.   Pardon, master:
I will be correspondent[74] to command,
And do my spriting gently.
    Pros.   Do so; and after two days
I will discharge thee.
    Ari.   That's my noble master !
What shall I do? say what; what shall I do?
    Pros. Go make thyself like to a nymph o' the sea:
Be subject to no sight but mine; invisible
To every eyeball else.   Go take this shape,

[74] *Correspondent* for *responsive;* that is, *obedient,* or *submissive.*

And hither come in't : hence, with diligence ! —

                            [*Exit* ARIEL.

Awake, dear heart, awake ! thou hast slept well ;
Awake !

   Mira. [*Waking.*]   The strangeness of your story put
Heaviness in me.

   Pros.   Shake it off.   Come on ;
We'll visit Caliban my slave, who never
Yields us kind answer.

   Mira.   'Tis a villain, sir,
I do not love to look on.

   Pros.   But, as 'tis,
We cannot miss him :[75] he does make our fire,
Fetch in our wood, and serves in offices
That profit us. — What, ho ! slave ! Caliban !
Thou earth, thou ! speak.

   Cal. [*Within.*]   There's wood enough within.

   Pros. Come forth, I say ! there's other business for thee :
Come forth, thou tortoise ! when ![76] —

       Re-enter ARIEL, *like a Water-nymph.*

Fine apparition !   My quaint[77] Ariel,
Hark in thine ear.

   Ari.   My lord, it shall be done.   [*Exit.*

   Pros. Thou poisonous slave, come forth !

          Enter CALIBAN.

   Cal. As wicked dew[78] as e'er my mother brush'd

   [75] Cannot *do without* him, or cannot *spare* him. So in Lyly's *Euphues :*
" Honey and wax, both so necessary that we cannot *miss* them."

   [76] *When !* was in common use as an exclamation of impatience.

   [77] *Ingenious, artful, adroit,* are old meanings of *quaint.*

   [78] " *Wicked* dew " is, probably, dew that has been *cursed,* and so made
poisonous or *baleful.* See Critical Notes.

With raven's feather from unwholesome fen
Drop on you both ! a south-west blow on ye,
And blister you all o'er ! [79]

Pros. For this, be sure, to-night thou shalt have cramps,
Side-stitches that shall pen thy breath up ; urchins [80]
Shall, for that vast [81] of night that they may work,
All exercise on thee ; thou shalt be pinch'd
As thick as honeycomb, each pinch more stinging
Than bees that made 'em. [82]

Cal.   I must eat my dinner.
This island's mine, by Sycorax my mother,
Which thou takest from me.   When thou camest here first,
Thou strokedst me, and madest much of me ; wouldst give me
Water with berries in't ; [83] and teach me how
To name the bigger light, and how the less,
That burn by day and night : and then I loved thee,
And show'd thee all the qualities o' the isle,
The fresh springs, brine-pits, barren place, and fertile :

[79] The Poet repeatedly ascribes a blighting virulence to the south-west wind ; perhaps because, in England, that wind often comes charged with the breath of the Gulf-stream. So he has " the south-fog rot him ! " and "all the contagion of the south light on you ! "

[80] *Urchins* were fairies of a particular class. Hedgehogs were also called *urchins ;* and it is probable that the sprites were so named, because they were of a mischievous kind, the *urchin* being anciently deemed a very noxious animal.

[81] So in *Hamlet*, i. 2, " in the dead *vast* and middle of the night " ; meaning the silent void or vacancy of night, when spirits were anciently supposed to walk abroad on errands of love or sport or mischief.

[82] *Honeycomb* is here regarded as plural, probably in reference to the *cells* of which honeycomb is composed.

[83] It does not well appear what this was. Coffee was known, but, I think, not used, in England in Shakespeare's time. Burton, in his *Anatomy of Melancholy*, 1632, has the following : " The Turks have a drink called *coffa*, so named of a *berry* as black as soot, and as bitter."

Cursèd be I that did so !   All the charms
Of Sycorax, toads, beetles, bats, light on you !
For I am all the subjects that you have,
Which first was mine own king: and here you sty me
In this hard rock, whiles you do keep from me
The rest o' the island.

   Pros.   Thou most lying slave,
Whom stripes may move, not kindness, I have used thee,
Filth as thou art, with human care ; and lodged thee
In mine own cell, till thou didst seek to violate
The honour of my child.

   Cal. O ho, O ho ! would 't had been done !
Thou didst prevent me ; I had peopled else
This isle with Calibans.

   Pros.   Abhorrèd slave,
Which any print of goodness wilt not take,
Being capable of all ill !   I pitied thee,
Took pains to make thee speak, taught thee each hour
One thing or other : when thou didst not, savage,
Know thine own meaning,[84] but wouldst gabble like
A thing most brutish, I endow'd thy purposes
With words that made them known.   But thy vile race,
Though thou didst learn, had that in't which good natures
Could not abide to be with ; therefore wast thou

   [84] Did not attach any meaning to the sounds he uttered. — Coleridge remarks upon Caliban as follows : " Caliban is all earth, all condensed and
gross in feelings and images ; he has the dawnings of understanding, without reason or the moral sense ; and in him, as in some brute animals, this
advance to the intellectual faculties, without the moral sense, is marked by
the appearance of vice.   For it is in the primacy of the moral being only
that man is truly human ; in his intellectual powers he is certainly ap-
proached by the brutes ; and, man's whole system duly considered, those
powers cannot be viewed as other than means to an end, that is, morality."

Deservedly confined into this rock,
Who hadst deserved more than a prison.

Cal. You taught me language ; and my profit on't
Is, I know how to curse.   The red plague rid [85] you
For learning me your language !

Pros.   Hag-seed, hence !
Fetch us in fuel ; and be quick, thou'rt best,
To answer other business.   Shrugg'st thou, malice?
If thou neglect'st, or dost unwillingly
What I command, I'll rack thee with old [86] cramps,
Fill all thy bones with achès,[87] make thee roar,
That beasts shall tremble at thy din.

Cal.   No, pray thee. —
[*Aside.*] I must obey : his art is of such power,
It would control my dam's god, Setebos,[88]
And make a vassal of him.

Pros.   So, slave ; hence !

                              [*Exit* CALIBAN.

[85] *Rid* here means *destroy* or *dispatch*. So in *Richard the Second*, v. 4:
" I am the King's friend, and will *rid* his foe."—Touching the " red plague,"
Halliwell quotes from *Practise of Physicke*, 1605: " Three different kinds of
plague-sore are mentioned ; sometimes it is *red*, otherwhiles yellow, and
sometimes blacke, which is the very worst and most venimous."

[86] *Old* was much used simply as an intensive, just as *huge* often is now.
The Poet has it repeatedly. See *The Merchant*, page 181, note 2.

[87] *Ache* was formerly pronounced like the letter *H*. The plural, *aches*,
was accordingly two syllables. We have many instances of such pronunciation in the old writers. So in *Antony and Cleopatra*, iv. 7: " I had a wound
here that was like a T, but now 'tis made an H." It is said that Kemble
the actor undertook to revive the old pronunciation of *aches* on the stage ;
but the audience would not stand it, and hissed him out of it.

[88] *Setebos* was the name of an American god, or rather devil, worshipped
by the Patagonians. In Eden's *History of Travaile*, 1577, is an account of
Magellan's voyage to the South Pole, containing a description of this god
and his worshippers ; wherein the author says : " When they felt the shackles
put upon their legs, they began to doubt ; but the captain did put them in

Re-enter ARIEL *invisible, playing and singing;* FERDINAND
following.

ARIEL'S SONG.

Come unto these yellow sands,
    And then take hands :
Curtsied when you have, and kiss'd
    The wild waves whist,[89]
Foot it featly here and there ;
And, sweet sprites, the burden bear.

Hark, hark !	*Burden dispersedly.*
The watch-dogs bark :	Bow-wow.
Hark, hark ! I hear	Bow-wow.
The strain of strutting chanticleer.	Cock-a-diddle-dow.

Ferd. Where should this music be? i' the air, or th'
    earth?
It sounds no more : and, sure, it waits upon
Some god o' the island.   Sitting on a bank,
Weeping again the King my father's wreck,
This music crept by me upon the waters,
Allaying both their fury and my passion[90]
With its sweet air : thence I have follow'd it,
Or it hath drawn me rather.   But 'tis gone.
No, it begins again.

ARIEL *sings.*

Full fathom five thy father lies ;
    Of his bones are coral made ;

comfort and bade them stand still. In fine, when they saw how they were
deceived, they roared like bulls, and cryed upon their *great devil Setebos*, to
help them."
    [89] Soothed or charmed the raging waters into stillness or peace.
    [90] *Passion* is here used in its proper Latin sense of *suffering*.

Those are pearls that were his eyes:
   Nothing of him that doth fade
But doth suffer a sea-change [91]
Into something rich and strange.
Sea-nymphs hourly ring his knell:
   Burden.   Ding-dong.
Hark! now I hear them, — Ding-dong, bell.

Ferd. The ditty does remember my drown'd father.
This is no mortal business, nor no sound
That the Earth owes.[92] I hear it now above me.

   Pros. The fringèd curtains of thine eye advance,[93]
And say what thou see'st yond.

   Mira.   What is't? a spirit?
Lord, how it looks about! Believe me, sir,
It carries a brave [94] form. But 'tis a spirit.

   Pros. No, wench;[95] it eats and sleeps, and hath such senses
As we have, such. This gallant which thou see'st
Was in the wreck; and, but he's something stain'd

[91] Nothing fades *without undergoing* a sea-change. This use of *but* occurs repeatedly. So in *Hamlet*, i. 3: "Do not sleep *but let* me hear from you;" that is, "*without letting* me hear." See, also, *Macbeth*, page 99, note 6.

[92] *Owe* is *own, possess.* The old form of the word was *owen.* Abbott, in his *Shakespeare Grammar*, has the following: "In the general destruction of inflections which prevailed during the Elizabethan period, *en* was particularly discarded. So strong was the discarding tendency, that even the *n* in *owen*, to *possess*, was dropped, and Shakespeare continually uses *owe* for *owen*, or *own.* The *n* has now been restored."

[93] *Advance*, here, is *raise* or *lift up.* So in *Romeo and Juliet*, ii. 3: "Ere the Sun *advance* his burning eye." Especially used of lifting up military standards.

[94] *Brave*, again, for *fine* or *superb.* See page 48, note 2.

[95] *Wench* was often used thus as a term of playful familiarity, without implying any thing of reproach or contempt.

With grief, that's beauty's canker,[96] thou mightst call him
A goodly person : he hath lost his fellows,
And strays about to find 'em.

    Mira.   I might call him
A thing divine ; for nothing natural
I ever saw so noble.

    Pros. [*Aside.*] It goes on, I see,
As my soul prompts it. — Spirit, fine spirit ! I'll free thee
Within two days for this.

    Ferd.   Most sure, the goddess
On whom these airs attend ! — Vouchsafe my prayer
May know if you remain upon this island ;
And that you will some good instruction give
How I may bear me here : my prime request,
Which I do last pronounce, is, — O you wonder ! —
If you be maid[97] or no ?

    Mira.   No wonder, sir ;
But certainly a maid.

    Ferd.   ·   My language ! Heavens ! —
I am the best of them that speak this speech,
Were I but where 'tis spoken.

    Pros.   How ! the best?
What wert thou, if the King of Naples heard thee?

    Ferd. A single thing,[98] as I am now, that wonders

---

[96] Shakespeare uses *canker* in four distinct senses, — the *canker-worm*, the *dog-rose*, a malignant sore, *cancer*, and *rust* or *tarnish*. Here it probably means the last; as in St. James, v. 3: "Your gold and silver is *cankered;* and the *rust* of them shall be a witness against you."

[97] Ferdinand has already spoken of Miranda as a goddess : he now asks, if she be a mortal; not a celestial being, but a maiden. Of course her answer is to be taken in the same sense as his question. The name *Miranda* literally signifies *wonderful.*

[98] The Poet repeatedly uses *single* for *weak* or *feeble:* here, along with

To hear thee speak of Naples.   He does hear me ;
And that he does I weep : myself am Naples ;
Who with mine eyes, ne'er since at ebb, beheld
The King my father wreck'd.

   Mira.   Alack, for mercy !
   Ferd.   Yes, faith, and all his lords ; the Duke of Milan
And his brave son[99] being twain.

   Pros.   [*Aside.*]   The Duke of Milan
And his more braver daughter could control thee,[100]
If now 'twere fit to do't.   At the first sight
They have changed eyes. — Delicate Ariel,
I'll set thee free for this ! — A word, good sir ;
I fear you've done yourself some wrong :[101] a word.

   Mira.   Why speaks my father so ungently?   This
Is the third man that e'er I saw ; the first
That e'er I sigh'd for : pity move my father
To be inclined my way !

   Ferd.   O, if a virgin,   .
And your affection not gone forth, I'll make you
The Queen of Naples.

   Pros.   Soft, sir ! one word more. —
[*Aside.*]   They're both in either's powers : but this swift
      business
I must uneasy make, lest too light winning

this, it has the further sense of *solitary* or *companionless*. Ferdinand sup-
poses himself to be the only one saved of all that were in the ship.

   [99] This young man, the son of Antonio, nowhere appears in the play, nor
is there any other mention of him.

   [100] To *control* was formerly used in the sense of to *refute;* from the French
contre-roller, to exhibit a *contrary account.* Prospero means that he could
refute what Ferdinand has just said about the Duke of Milan.

   [101] " Done wrong to your character, in claiming to be King of Naples."
Or incurred the penalty of being a spy or an usurper, by assuming a title
that does not belong to him.

Make the prize light.[102] — One word more ; I charge thee
That thou attend me : Thou dost here usurp
The name thou owest not ; and hast put thyself
Upon this island as a spy, to win it
From me, the lord on't.

    Ferd.   No, as I'm a man.

    Mira. There's nothing ill can dwell in such a temple :
If the ill spirit have so fair a house,
Good things will strive to dwell with't.

    Pros. [*To* FERD.]   Follow me. —
Speak not you for him ; he's a traitor. — Come ;
I'll manacle thy neck and feet together :
Sea-water shalt thou drink ; thy food shall be
The fresh-brook muscles, wither'd roots, and husks
Wherein the acorn cradled : follow.

    Ferd.   No ;
I will resist such entertainment, till
Mine enemy has more power.

               [*He draws, and is charmed from moving.*

    Mira.   O dear father,
Make not too rash a trial of him, for
He's gentle, and not fearful.[103]

    Pros.   What, I say,
My fool my tutor ! — Put thy sword up, traitor ;

[102] In this scene, as it proceeds, is displayed the impression made by
Ferdinand and Miranda on each other; it is love at first sight, — " at the
first sight they have changed eyes." Prospero's interruption of the court-
ship has often seemed to me to have no sufficient motive; still, his alleged
reason, " lest too light winning make the prize light," is enough for the
ethereal connections of the romantic imagination, although it would not be
so for the historical. — COLERIDGE.

[103] This clearly means that Ferdinand is brave and high-spirited, so that,
if pressed too hard, he will rather die than succumb. It is a good old notion
that bravery and gentleness naturally go together.

Who makest a show, but darest not strike, thy conscience
Is so possess'd with guilt : come from thy ward ; [104]
For I can here disarm thee with this stick,
And make thy weapon drop.

    Mira.   Beseech you, father ! —
    Pros. Hence ! hang not on my garments.
    Mira.   Sir, have pity ;
I'll be his surety.
    P.·os.   Silence ! one word more
Shall make me chide thee, if not hate thee.   What !
An advocate for an impostor ? hush !
Thou think'st there are no more such shapes as he,
Having seen but him and Caliban : foolish wench !
To th' most of men this is a Caliban,
And they to him are angels.

    Mira.   My affections
Are, then, most humble ; I have no ambition
To see a goodlier man.

    Pros. [*To* FERD.]   Come on ; obey :
Thy nerves [105] are in their infancy again,
And have no vigour in them.

    Ferd.   So they are :
My spirits, as in a dream, are all bound up.
My father's loss, the weakness which I feel,
The wreck of all my friends, and this man's threats
To whom I am subdued, are light to me,
Might I but through my prison once a day

---

    [104] *Ward* is *posture* or *attitude of defence.* Ferdinand is standing with
his sword drawn, and his body planted, ready for defending himself. So, in
1 Henry the Fourth, ii. 4, Falstaff says, "Thou knowest my old *ward :*
here I lay, and thus I bore my point."

    [105] *Nerves* for *sinews ;* the two words being used indifferently in the
Poet's time. See *Hamlet,* page 80, note 20.

Behold this maid : all corners else o' the Earth
Let liberty make use of; space enough
Have I in such a prison.

   Pros. [*Aside.*] It works. — [*To* FERD.] Come on. —
Thou hast done well, fine Ariel ! — Follow me. —
[*To* ARIEL.] Hark, what thou else shalt do me.

   Mira.   Be of comfort ; [106]
My father's of a better nature, sir,
Than he appears by speech : this is unwonted
Which now came from him.

   Pros. [*To* ARIEL.]   Thou shalt be as free
As mountain winds : but then exactly do
All points of my command.

   Ari. ·   To th' syllable.

   Pros. Come, follow. — Speak not for him.   [*Exeunt.*

ACT II.

SCENE I. — *Another part of the Island.*

Enter ALONSO, SEBASTIAN, ANTONIO, GONZALO, ADRIAN, FRAN-
CISCO, *and Others.*

   Gonza. Beseech you, sir, be merry : you have cause —
So have we all — of joy ; for our escape
Is much beyond our loss.   Our hint of woe
Is common ; every day some sailor's wife,
The master of some merchant,[1] and the merchant,
Have just our theme of woe : but for the miracle —

   [106] "Be *of comfort*" is old language for be *comforted.*
   [1] It was usual to call a *merchant-vessel* a *merchant;* as we now say a *mer-
chant-man.*

I mean our preservation — few in millions
Can speak like us : then wisely, good sir, weigh
Our sorrow with our comfort.

    Alon.   Pr'ythee, peace. '

    Sebas. He receives comfort like cold porridge.

    Anto. The visitor[2] will not give him o'er so.

    Sebas. Look, he's winding up the watch of his wit ; by-and-by it will strike.

    Gonza. Sir, —

    Sebas. One : — tell.[3]

    Gonza. — When every grief is entertain'd that's offer'd, Comes to the entertainer —

    Sebas. A dollar.

    Gonza. Dolour comes to him, indeed : you have spoken truer than you purposed.

    Sebas. You have taken it wiselier than I meant you should.

    Gonza. Therefore, my lord, —

    Anto. Fie, what a spendthrift is he of his tongue !

    Alon. I pr'ythee, spare me.

    Gonza. Well, I have done : but yet —

    Sebas. He will be talking.

    Anto. Which, of he or Adrian,[4] for a good wager, first begins to crow ?

    [2] He calls Gonzalo a *visitor* in allusion to the office of one who visits the sick or the afflicted, to give counsel and consolation. The caustic scoffing humour of Sebastian and Antonio, in this scene, is wisely conceived. See the Introduction, page 29.

    [3] *Tell* is *count*, or *keep tally;* referring to " the watch of his wit," which he was said to be "winding up," and which now begins to strike. See *King Lear*, page 115, note 10.

    [4] This, it appears, is an old mode of speech, which is now entirely obsolete. Shakespeare has it once again in *A Midsummer-Night's Dream*, iii. 2: " Now follow, if thou darest, to try whose right, *of thine or mine*, is most in

Sebas. The old cock.

Anto. The cockerel.

Sebas. Done ! The wager?

Anto. A laughter.

Sebas. A match !

Adri. Though this island seem to be desert, —

Sebas. Ha, ha, ha ! — So, you're paid.[5]

Adri. — uninhabitable, and almost inaccessible, —

Sebas. Yet —

Adri. — yet —

Anto. He could not miss't.

Adri. — it must needs be of subtle, tender, and delicate temperance.[6]

Anto. Temperance was a delicate wench.

Sebas. Ay, and a subtle ; as he most learnedly delivered.

Adri. The air breathes upon us here most sweetly.

Sebas. As if it had lungs, and rotten ones.

Anto. Or as 'twere perfumed by a fen.

Gonza. Here is every thing advantageous to life.

Anto. True ; save means to live.

Sebas. Of that there's none, or little.

Gonza. How lush[7] and lusty the grass looks ! how green !

Anto. The ground, indeed, is tawny.

Helena." And Walker quotes an apposite passage from Sidney's *Arcadia :*
" The question arising, who should be the first to fight against Phalantus,
of the black or the ill-apparelled knight," &c.

[5] A laugh having been agreed upon as the wager, and Sebastian having
lost, he now pays with a laugh.

[6] By *temperance* Adrian means *temperature*, and Antonio plays upon the
word ; alluding, perhaps, to the Puritan custom of bestowing the names of
the cardinal virtues upon their children.

[7] *Lush* is *juicy, succulent,* — luxuriant.

Sebas. With an eye of green in't.[8]

Anto. He misses not much.

Sebas. No ; he doth but mistake the truth totally.

Gonza. But the rarity of it is, — which is indeed almost beyond credit, —

Sebas. As many vouch'd rarities are.

Gonza. — that our garments, being, as they were, drenched in the sea, hold, notwithstanding, their freshness and gloss, being rather new-dyed than stain'd with salt water.

Anto. If but one of his pockets could speak, would it not say he lies?

Sebas. Ay, or very falsely pocket up his report.

Gonza. Methinks our garments are now as fresh as when we put them on first in Afric, at the marriage of the King's fair daughter Claribel to the King of Tunis.

Sebas. 'Twas a sweet marriage, and we prosper well in our return.

Adri. Tunis was never graced before with such a paragon to[9] their Queen.

Gonza. Not since widow Dido's time.

Anto. Widow? a pox o' that ! How came that widow in? Widow Dido !

Sebas. What if he had said widower Æneas too? Good Lord, how you take it !

Adri. Widow Dido, said you? you make me study of that : she was of Carthage, not of Tunis.

---

[8] A *tint* or *shade* of green. So in Sandy's *Travels :* "Cloth of silver, tissued with an *eye* of green;" and Bayle says: "Red with an *eye* of blue makes a purple."

[9] *To* was continually used in such cases where we should use *for* or *as*. So in the Marriage Office of the Church: "Wilt thou have this woman *to* thy wedded wife?" Also, in St. Mark, xii. 23: "The seven had her *to* wife."

Gonza. This Tunis, sir, was Carthage.

Adri. Carthage !

Gonza. I assure you, Carthage.

Anto. His word is more than the miraculous harp.[10]

Sebas. He hath raised the wall and houses too.

Anto. What impossible matter will he make easy next?

Sebas. I think he will carry this island home in his pocket, and give it his son for an apple.

Anto. And, sowing the kernels of it in the sea, bring forth more islands.

Alon. Ah !

Anto. Why, in good time.

Gonza. Sir, we were talking that our garments seem now as fresh as when we were at Tunis at the marriage of your daughter, who is now Queen.

Anto. And the rarest that e'er came there.

Sebas. Bate, I beseech you, widow Dido.

Anto. O, widow Dido ! ay, widow Dido.

Gonza. Is not, sir, my doublet as fresh as the first day I wore it ? I mean, in a sort.

Anto. That sort was well fish'd for.[11]

Gonza. When I wore it at your daughter's marriage?

Alon. You cram these words into mine ears against The stomach of my sense.[12]   Would I had never

[10] Amphion, King of Thebes, was a prodigious musician : god Mercury gave him a lyre, with which he charmed the stones into their places, and thus built the walls of the city : as Wordsworth puts it, " The gift to King Amphion, that wall'd a city with its melody."   Tunis is in fact supposed to be on or near the site of ancient Carthage.

[11] A punning allusion, probably, to one of the meanings of *sort*, which was *lot* or *portion ;* from the Latin *sors.*

[12] That is, " when the state of my feelings does not relish them, or has no *appetite* for them."   *Stomach* for *appetite* occurs repeatedly.

Married my daughter there! for, coming thence,
My son is lost; and, in my rate,[13] she too,
Who is so far from Italy removed,
I ne'er again shall see her.   O thou mine heir
Of Naples and of Milan, what strange fish
Hath made his meal on thee?

   Fran.   Sir, he may live:
I saw him beat the surges under him,
And ride upon their backs; he trod the water,
Whose enmity he flung aside, and breasted
The surge most swoln that met him: his bold head
'Bove the contentious waves he kept, and oar'd
Himself with his good arms in lusty stroke
To th' shore, that o'er his [14] wave-worn basis bow'd,
As [15] stooping to relieve him: I not doubt
He came alive to land.

   Alon.   No, no; he's gone.

   Sebas. Sir, you may thank yourself for this great loss,
That would not bless our Europe with your daughter,
But rather lose her to an African;
Where she at least is banish'd from your eye,
Who [16] hath cause to wet the grief on't.

---

[13] *Rate* for *reckoning, account,* or *estimation.*

[14] *His* for *its,* referring to *shore.* In the Poet's time *its* was not an accepted word: it was then just creeping into use; and he has it occasionally, especially in his later plays; as it occurs once or twice in this play. It does not occur once in the Bible as printed in 1611.

[15] Here *as* is put for *as if;* a very frequent usage with the Poet, as also with other writers of the time.

[16] *Who* and *which* were used indifferently both of persons and things. Here *who* refers to *eye.* And the meaning probably is, "your eye, which hath cause to sprinkle or water your grief with tears." This would of course make the grief grow stronger. "The grief *on't*" is the grief *arising from it* or *out of it;* that is, from the loss or banishment of Claribel.

Alon.   Pr'ythee, peace.

Sebas. You were kneel'd to, and impórtuned otherwise,
By all of us ; and the fair soul herself
Weigh'd, between loathness and obedience, at
Which end the beam should bow.[17] We've lost your son,
I fear, for ever : Milan and Naples have
More widows in them of this business' making
Than we bring men to comfort them : the fault's
Your own.

    Alon.   So is the dear'st o' the loss.[18]

    Gonza.   My lord Sebastian

The truth you speak doth lack some gentleness,
And time to speak it in : you rub the sore,
When you should bring the plaster.

    Sebas.   Very well.

    Anto. And most chirurgeonly.[19]

    Gonza. It is foul weather in us all, good sir,
When you are cloudy.[20]

    Sebas.   Foul weather !

    Anto.   Very foul.

    Gonza. Had I plantation[21] of this isle, my lord, —

    Anto. He'd sow't with nettle-seed.

---

[17] *Hesitated*, or *stood in doubt*, between *reluctance* and obedience, which way the balance should turn or incline. To *weigh* is to *deliberate*, and hence to pause, to be *in suspense*, or to suspend action.

[18] *Dear* was used of any thing that causes strong feeling, whether of pleasure or of pain ; as it *hurts* us to lose that which is *dear* to us. So that here the sense is, the *worst* or *heaviest* of the loss.

[19] *Chirurgeon* is the old word, which has got transformed into *surgeon*.

[20] The meaning is, "your *gloom* makes us all gloomy." A cloud in the face is a common metaphor both for anger and for sorrow.

[21] In Shakespeare's time a *plantation* meant a *colony*, and was so used of the American colonies. Here *plantation* is a " verbal noun," and means *the colonising*.

Sebas.   Or docks, or mallows.

Gonza. — And were the King on't, what would I do?

Sebas. 'Scape being drunk for want of wine.

Gonza. I' the commonwealth I would by contraries
Execute all things : for no kind of traffic
Would I admit ; no name of magistrate ;
Letters should not be known ; riches, poverty,
And use of service, none ; contract, succession,
Bourn, bound of land, tilth,[22] vineyard, none ;
No use of metal, corn, or wine, or oil ;
No occupation ; all men idle, all,
And women too, but innocent and pure ;
No sovereignty : —

Sebas.   Yet he would be king on't.

Anto. The latter end of his commonwealth forgets the
beginning.

Gonza. — All things in common Nature should produce
Without sweat or endeavour : treason, felony,
Sword, pike, knife, gun, or need of any engine,[23]
Would I not have ; but Nature should bring forth,
Of its own kind, all foison,[24] all abundance,
To feed my innocent people.

Sebas. No marrying 'mong his subjects?

Anto. None, man ; all idle, — trulls and knaves.

[22] *Succession* is the tenure of property by inheritance, as the son *succeeds* the father. — *Bourn* is *boundary* or *limit.* Properly it means a stream of water, river, rivulet, or brook ; these being the most natural boundaries of landed property. — *Tilth* is *tillage :* also used of land tilled, or prepared for sowing. So in *Measure for Measure,* iv. 1 : " Our corn's to reap, for yet our *tilth's* to sow."

[23] *Engine* was applied to any kind of *machine :* here it probably means *furniture of war.*

[24] *Foison* is an old word for *plenty* or *abundance* of provision, especially of the fruits of the soil. Often used so by the Poet.

Gonza. I would with such perfection govern, sir,
T' excel the golden age.[25]

Sebas.   God save his Majesty !

Anto. Long live Gonzalo !

Gonza.   And, — do you mark me, sir? —

Alon. Pr'ythee, no more : thou dost talk nothing to me.

Gonza. I do well believe your Highness ; and did it to
minister occasion to these gentlemen, who are of such sensible[26] and nimble lungs, that they always use to laugh at
nothing.

Anto. 'Twas you we laugh'd at.

Gonza. Who in this kind of merry fooling am nothing to
you :[27] so you may continue, and laugh at nothing still.

Anto. What a blow was there given !

Sebas. An it had not fallen flat-long.[28]

Gonza. You are gentlemen of brave mettle ;[29] you would
lift the Moon out of her sphere, if she would[30] continue in it
five weeks without changing.

[25] " The golden age " is that fabulous period in " the dark backward of
time " when men knew nothing of sin and sorrow, and were so wise and
good as to have no need of laws and government. Milton, in his *Ode on the
Nativity*, has " Time will run back, and fetch the *age of gold*."

[26] *Sensible* for *sensitive* or *ticklish*. So in *Coriolanus*, i. 3 : " I would your
cambric were *sensible* as your finger, that you might leave pricking it for
pity." See, also, *Hamlet*, page 109, note 44.

[27] Nothing *in comparison with* you. So the Poet often uses *to*.

[28] The idea is of a sword handled so awkwardly as to hit with the side,
and not with the edge.

[29] *Brave mettle* is *high, glorious*, or *magnificent spirit*. The Poet often
has *mettle* in that sense. — *Sphere*, in the next line, is *orbit*.

[30] Our present usage requires *should*. In Shakespeare's time, the auxil-
iaries *could, should*, and *would* were often used indiscriminately, as were
also *shall* and *will*. So a little further on : " Methinks I see it in thy face,
what thou *shouldst* be "; *shouldst* for *wouldst*. Again, later in this scene,
" *should* not upbraid our course "; *should* for *would*. Also, " who *shall* be
of as little memory "; *shall* for *will*.

Enter ARIEL, *invisible, playing solemn music.*

Sebas. We would so, and then go a-bat-fowling.[31]

Anto. Nay, good my lord, be not angry.

Gonza. No, I warrant you; I will not adventure my discretion[32] so weakly. Will you laugh me asleep? for I am very heavy.

Anto. Go sleep, and hear us not.

                 [*All sleep but* ALON., SEBAS., *and* ANTO.

Alon. What, all so soon asleep! I wish mine eyes
Would, with themselves, shut up my thoughts: I find
They are inclined to do so.

Sebas.   Please you, sir,
Do not omit the heavy offer of it: [33]
It seldom visits sorrow; when it doth,
It is a comforter.

Anto.   We two, my lord,
Will guard your person while you take your rest,
And watch your safety.

Alon.   Thank you. — Wondrous heavy.

               [ALONSO *sleeps. Exit* ARIEL.

Sebas. What a strange drowsiness possesses them!

Anto. It is the quality o' the climate.

Sebas.   Why
Doth it not, then, our eyelids sink? I find not

---

[31] *Bat-fowling* was a term used of catching birds in the night. Fielding, in *Joseph Andrews*, calls it *bird-batting*, and says " it is performed by holding a large clap-net before a lantern, and at the same time beating the bushes; for the birds, when they are disturbed from their places of rest or roost, immediately make to the light, and so are enticed within the net."

[32] That is, " hazard my character for discretion, or put it in peril."

[33] " Do not *slight* or *neglect* the *offer of sleep* which it holds out," or " when it offers to make you sleepy." *Heavy* is here used proleptically, or *anticipatively*. See *Macbeth*, page 113, note 11.

Myself disposed to sleep.

   Anto.   Nor I ; my spirits are nimble.
They fell together all, as by consent ;
They dropp'd, as by a thunder-stroke.   What might,
Worthy Sebastian, O, what might !³⁴   No more :
And yet methinks I see it in thy face,
What thou shouldst be : th' occasion speaks thee ;³⁵ and
My strong imagination sees a crown
Dropping upon thy head.

   Sebas.   What, art thou waking?

   Anto. Do you not hear me speak?

   Sebas.   I do ; and surely
It is a sleepy language, and thou speak'st
Out of thy sleep.   What is it thou didst say?
This is a strange repose, to be asleep
With eyes wide open ; standing, speaking, moving,
And yet so fast asleep.

   Anto.   Noble Sebastian,
Thou lett'st thy fortune sleep, — die rather ; wink'st
Whiles thou art waking.³⁶

   Sebas.   Thou dost snore distinctly ;
There's meaning in thy snores.

   Anto. I am more serious than my custom : you
Must be so too, if heed me ; which to do
Trebles thee o'er.³⁷

    ³⁴ "What might *you be !*" is probably the meaning.
    ³⁵ *Reveals* or *proclaims* thee.   Such an opportunity kindles the devil in
Sebastian, and makes his ambitious thoughts legible in his face.   So in
Macbeth, i. 5 : "Your face is as a book where men may read strange matters."
    ³⁶ " Closest thine eyes as if asleep while thou art awake."   *While, whiles,*
and *whilst* were used indifferently.
    ³⁷ " The doing of which will make thee thrice what thou art now."

Sebas.   Well, I am standing water.[38]

Anto. I'll teach you how to flow.

Sebas.   Do so : to ebb
Hereditary sloth instructs me.

Anto.   O,
If you but knew how you the purpose cherish
Whiles thus you mock it ! how, in stripping it,
You more invest it ![39] Ebbing men, indeed,
Most often do so near the bottom run
By their own fear or sloth.

Sebas.   Pr'ythee, say on :
The setting of thine eye and cheek proclaim
A matter from thee ; and a birth indeed
Which throes thee much to yield.[40]

Anto.   Thus, sir : —
Although this lord of weak remembrance, this,
Who shall be of as little memory[41]
When he is earth'd, hath here almost persuaded —
For he's a spirit of persuasion, only
Professes to persuade — the King his son's alive,
'Tis as impossible that he's undrown'd

[38] Water standing between ebb and flow, and so ready to be moved in either direction. So in *Twelfth Night*, i. 5: " 'Tis with him e'en *standing water* between boy and man."

[39] Sebastian shows that he both takes and welcomes Antonio's suggestion, by his making it a theme of jest; and the more he thus denudes the hint of obscurity by playing with it, the more he clothes it with his own approval.—"*Ebbing* men " are men whose fortunes are ebbing away or declining.

[40] " In the yielding of which you struggle very hard, and suffer much pain."—*Matter*, here, is *something of vast import.*

[41] *Will* be as little remembered, or as quickly forgotten, as he is apt to forget. *Weak remembrance* means *feeble memory.* Francisco is the lord referred to.—*Shall* for *will*, as noted a little before.

As he that sleeps here swims.

   Sebas.   I have no hope
That he's undrown'd.

   Anto.   O, out of that no hope
What great hope have you ! no hope that way is
Another way so high a hope, that even
Ambition cannot pierce a wink beyond, —
But doubt discovery there.[42]   Will you grant with me
That Ferdinand is drown'd?

   Sebas.   He's gone.

   Anto.   Then, tell me,
Who's the next heir of Naples?

   Sebas.   Claribel.

   Anto. She that is Queen of Tunis ; she that dwells
Ten leagues beyond man's life ;[43] she that from Naples
Can have no note,[44] unless the Sun were post, —
The Man-i'-the-moon's too slow, — till new-born chins
Be rough and razorable.   She 'twas for whom [45] we
All were sea-swallow'd, though some cast again ; [46]

[42] Cannot pierce so much beyond as may be measured by a wink of the eye ; *wink* meaning the same as *jot* or *atom*. Probably all are familiar with the word in that sense. — The last clause is obscure, or worse : probably, if the text be right, the force of *cannot* was meant to be continued over *But doubt*. See Critical Notes.

[43] Beyond a lifetime of travelling. Of course this passage is a piece of intentional hyperbole ; and Sebastian shows that he takes it so, by exclaiming, "What *stuff* is this ! "

[44] *Note* for *knowledge* or *notice*. See *King Lear*, page 128, note 3.

[45] *For whom* is here equivalent to *because of whom*, or *on whose account*. *For* is often used so. Antonio means, apparently, to imply that, inasmuch as Claribel has been the occasion of what has befallen them, they need not scruple to cut her off from the Neapolitan throne. And he goes on to intimate that, by the recent strange events, Sebastian and himself are marked out, as by destiny, for some mighty achievement or some peerless honour.

[46] The image is of being swallowed by the sea, and then cast up, or cast

And, by that destiny, to perform an act
Whereof what's past is prologue ; what to come,
In yours and my discharge.
   Sebas.   What stuff is this !   How say you?
'Tis true, my brother's daughter's Queen of Tunis ;
So is she heir of Naples ; 'twixt which regions
There is some space.
   Ant.   A space whose every cubit
Seems to cry out, *How shalt thou, Claribel,*
Measure us back to Naples ? [47]   *Keep in Tunis,*
And let Sebastian wake !   Say, this were death
That now hath seized them ; why, they were no worse
Than now they are.   There be that can rule Naples
As well as he that sleeps ; lords that can prate
As amply and unnecessarily
As this Gonzalo : I myself could make
A chough of as deep chat.[48]   O, that you bore
The mind that I do ! what a sleep were this
For your advancement !   Do you understand me?
   Sebas. Methinks I do.
   Anto.   And how does your content
Tender your own good fortune?[49]
   Sebas.   I remember
You did supplant your brother Prospero.
   Anto.   True :

ashore. — In the next line, " by that destiny " is by the same destiny through which they have so miraculously escaped drowning.

   [47] " Measure the distance back from Naples to us; " or "*return* to us."

   [48] Could *produce, breed,* or *train* a parrot to talk as wisely.   A *chough* is a bird of the jackdaw kind.

   [49] Obscure, again.   But the meaning seems to be, " How does your present *contentment,* that is, apathy or indifference, regard or look out for your own advantage or interest ? "   To *tender* a thing is to *take care of* it, or be *careful for* it.   See *Hamlet,* page 73, note 27.

And look how well my garments sit upon me ;
Much feater [50] than before : my brother's servants
Were then my fellows ; now they are my men.

    Sebas. But, for your conscience —

    Anto. Ay, sir ; and where lies that ? if 'twere a kibe,[51]
'Twould put me to my slipper : but I feel not
This deity in my bosom : twenty consciences,
That stand 'twixt me and Milan, candied [52] be they,
And melt, ere they molest ! Here lies your brother,
No better than the earth he lies upon,
If he were that which now he's like ; whom I,
With this obedient steel, three inches of it,
Can lay to bed for ever ; whiles you, doing thus,
To the perpetual wink for aye might put
This ancient morsel, this Sir Prudence, who
Should not upbraid our course. For all the rest,
They'll take suggestion [53] as a cat laps milk ;
They'll tell [54] the clock to any business that
We say befits the hour.

    Sebas.   Thy case, dear friend,
Shall be my precedent ; as thou gott'st Milan,

---

[50] *Feater* is *more finely*, or more *becomingly.* — *Fellows*, in the next line,
is *equals.* The word is often used in that sense.

[51] The Poet has *kibe* several times for the well-known heel-sore, an
ulcerated chilblain.

[52] *Candied*, here, is *congealed*, or *crystallized*. So in *Timon of Athens*,
iv. 3 : " Will the cold brook, *candied with ice*, caudle thy morning taste ? "

[53] *Suggest* and its derivatives were often used in the sense of to *tempt.*
Thus Shakespeare has such phrases as " tender youth is soon *suggested*,"
and " what serpent hath *suggested* thee." The meaning of the text is, " They'll
fall in with any temptation to villainy " ; *they* referring to the other lords
present.

[54] *Tell*, again, for *count.* The meaning is, " They'll speak whatever words
we choose to have them speak," or " put into their mouths."

I'll come by Naples.   Draw thy sword : one stroke
Shall free thee from the tribute which thou pay'st ;
And I the King shall [55] love thee.

 Anto.   Draw together ;
And when I rear my hand, do you the like,
To fall it on Gonzalo.

  Sebas.   O, but one word.

         [*They converse apart.*

   Music.   Re-enter ARIEL, *invisible.*

 Ari. My master through his art foresees the danger
That you, his friend, are in ; and sends me forth —
For else his project dies — to keep thee living.·

        [*Sings in* GONZALO'S *ear.*

   While you here do snoring lie,
   Open-eyed conspiracy
    His time doth take.
   If of life you keep a care,
   Shake off slumber, and beware :
    Awake ! awake !

 Anto. Then let us both be sudden.

  Gonza. [*Waking.*]   Now, good angels
Preserve the King ! — [*To* SEBAS. *and* ANTO.] Why, how
  now ! — [*To* ALON.] Ho, awake ! —
[*To* SEBAS. *and* ANTO.] Why are you drawn? wherefore
  this ghastly looking?

 Alon. [*Waking.*] What's the matter?

 Sebas. Whiles we stood here securing your repose,
Even now, we heard a hollow burst of bellowing
Like bulls, or rather lions : did't not wake you ?
It struck mine ear most terribly.

   [55] *Shall* for *will*, again.   See page 86, note 41.

Alon.   I heard nothing.

Anto. O, 'twas a din to fright a monster's ear,
To make an earthquake ! sure, it was the roar
Of a whole herd of lions.

Alon.   Heard you this, Gonzalo?

Gonza. Upon mine honour, sir, I heard a humming,
And that a strange one too, which did awake me :
I shaked you, sir, and cried : as mine eyes open'd,
I saw their weapons drawn : there was a noise,
That's verity. 'Tis best we stand upon our guard,
Or that we quit this place : let's draw our weapons.

Alon. Lead off this ground ; and let's make further search
For my poor son.

Gonza.   Heavens keep him from these beasts !
For he is, sure, i' the island.

Alon.   Lead away.

                              [*Exit with the others.*

Ari. Prospero my lord shall know what I have done :—
So, King, go safely on to seek thy son.   [*Exit.*

SCENE II. — *Another part of the Island.*

Enter CALIBAN, *with a burden of wood.   A noise of Thunder
heard.*

Cal. All the infections that the Sun sucks up
From bogs, fens, flats, on Prosper fall, and make him
By inch-meal[1] a disease !   His spirits hear me,
And yet I needs must curse.   But they'll nor pinch,
Fright me with urchin-shows,[2] pitch me i' the mire,

---

[1] *Inch-meal* and *limb-meal* were used just as we use *piece-meal*.

[2] *Urchin-shows* are *fairy*-shows ; as *urchin* was the name of a certain
description of fairies.   See page 66, note 80.

Nor lead me, like a fire-brand,[3] in the dark
Out of my way, unless he bid 'em : but
For every trifle are they set upon me ;
Sometime[4] like apes, that mow[5] and chatter at me,
And after bite me ; then like hedgehogs, which
Lie tumbling in my barefoot way, and mount
Their pricks[6] at my foot-fall ; sometime am I
All wound with adders, who with cloven tongues
Do hiss me into madness.   Lo, now, lo !
Here comes a spirit of his ; and to torment me
For bringing wood in slowly.   I'll fall flat ;
Perchance he will not mind me.

Enter TRINCULO.

Trin. Here's neither bush nor shrub, to bear off any
weather at all, and another storm brewing ; I hear it sing i'
the wind : yond same black cloud, yond huge one, looks like
a foul bombard[7] that would shed his liquor.   If it should
thunder as it did before, I know not where to hide my head :
yond same cloud cannot choose but fall by pailfuls. — What
have we here? a man or a fish?   Dead or alive?   A fish: he
smells like a fish ; a very ancient and fish-like smell ; a kind
of not-of-the-newest poor-john.[8]   A strange fish !   Were I in
England now, as once I was, and had but this fish painted,
not a holiday fool there but would give a piece of silver : there
would this monster make a man ; any strange beast there

---

[3] The *ignis fatuus* was thought to be the work of naughty spirits.
[4] *Sometime* and *sometimes* were used indiscriminately.
[5] To *mow* is to *make mouths.*   So Nash's *Pierce Penniless :* "Nobody at
home but an ape, that sat in the porch, and made mops and *mows* at him,"
[6] *Pricks* is the ancient word for *prickles.*
[7] A *bombard* is a black jack of leather, to hold beer, &c.
[8] *Poor-john* is an old name for *hake* salted and dried.

makes a man : [9] when they will not give a doit to relieve a lame beggar, they will lay out ten to see a dead Indian. Legg'd like a man ! and his fins like arms ! Warm, o' my troth ! I do now let loose my opinion ; hold it no longer : this is no fish, but an islander, that hath lately suffered by a thunderbolt. [*Thunder.*] Alas, the storm is come again ! my best way is to creep under his gaberdine ; [10] there is no other shelter hereabout : misery acquaints a man with strange bed-fellows. I will here shroud till the dregs of the storm be past.   [*Creeps under* CALIBAN'S *garment.*

Enter STEPHANO, *singing ; a bottle in his hand.*

Steph.   . *I shall no more to sea, to sea,*
                 Here shall I die ashore ; —

This is a very scurvy tune to sing at a man's funeral : well, here's my comfort.   [*Drinks.*

[Sings.] *The master, the swabber,*[11] *the boatswain, and I,*
              The gunner, and his mate,
          Loved Mall, Meg, and Marian, and Margery,
              But none of us cared for Kate ;
          For she had a tongue with a tang,[12]
          Would cry to a sailor, Go hang !
          She loved not the savour of tar nor of pitch :
          Then to sea, boys, and let her go hang !

---

[9] Sets a man up, or *makes his fortune.* The phrase was often used thus. So in *A Midsummer-Night's Dream*, iv. 2 : " If our sport had gone forward, we had all been *made men.*"

[10] A *gaberdine* was a coarse outer garment. "A shepherd's pelt, frock, or *gaberdine*, such a coarse long jacket as our porters wear over the rest of their garments," says Cotgrave. "A kind of rough cassock or frock like an Irish mantle," says Philips.

[11] A *swabber* is one whose special business it is to sweep, mop, or *swab* the deck of a ship.

[12] *Tang* was used of what has a pungent or biting taste or flavour.

This is a scurvy tune too : but here's my comfort. [*Drinks.*

Cal. Do not torment me : — O !

Steph. What's the matter? Have we devils here? Do you put tricks upon's with savages and men of Inde, ha?[13] I have not 'scaped drowning, to be afeard now of your four legs; for it hath been said, As proper a man as ever went on four legs cannot make him give ground ; and it shall be said so again, while Stephano breathes at's nostrils.

Cal. The spirit torments me : — O !

Steph. This is some monster of the isle with four legs, who hath got, as I take it, an ague. Where the Devil should he learn our language? I will give him some relief, if it be but for that. If I can recover him, and keep him tame, and get to Naples with him, he's a present for any emperor that ever trod on neat's-leather.[14]

Cal. Do not torment me, pr'ythee :
I'll bring my wood home faster.

Steph. He's in his fit now, and does not talk after the wisest. He shall taste of my bottle : if he have never drunk wine afore, it will go near to remove his fit. If I can recover him, and keep him tame, I will not take too much for him : [15] he shall pay for him that hath him, and that soundly.

Cal. Thou dost me yet but little hurt ;
Thou wilt anon, I know it by thy trembling :
Now Prosper works upon thee.

Steph. Come on your ways ; open your mouth ; here is

---

[13] Alluding, probably, to the impostures practised by showmen, who often exhibited sham wonders pretended to be brought from America. *Inde* for *India*, East or West.

[14] *Neat* is an old epithet for all cattle of the bovine genus. So that *neat's-leather* is *cowhide* or *calfskin.* So in *The Winter's Tale*, i. 2: "And yet the steer, the heifer, and the calf are all called *neat*."

[15] A piece of vulgar irony, meaning, "I'll take as much as I can get."

that which will give language to you, cat:[16] open your mouth; this will shake your shaking, I can tell you, and that soundly: [*Gives him drink.*] you cannot tell who's your friend; open your chops again.   [*Gives him more drink.*

Trin. I should know that voice: it should be — but he is drown'd; and these are devils: — O, defend me!

Steph. Four legs, and two voices, — a most delicate monster? His forward voice now is to speak well of his friend; his backward voice is to utter foul speeches and to detract. If all the wine in my bottle will recover him, I will help his ague: [*Gives him drink.*] — Come, — Amen![17] I will pour some in thy other mouth.

Trin. Stephano!

Steph. Doth thy other mouth call me? — Mercy, mercy! This is a devil, and no monster: I will leave him; I have no long spoon.

Trin. Stephano! — If thou be'st Stephano, touch me, and speak to me; for I am Trinculo, — be not afeard, — thy good friend Trinculo.

Steph. If thou be'st Trinculo, come forth: I'll pull thee by the lesser legs: if any be Trinculo's legs, these are they. [*Pulls* TRINCULO *out.*] Thou art very Trinculo[18] indeed! How camest thou to be the siege of this moon-calf?[19]

---

[16] Shakespeare gives his characters appropriate language: "They belch forth proverbs in their drink," "Good liquor will *make a cat speak,*" and "He who eats with the devil had need of a *long spoon.*"

[17] Stephano is frightened, and put to his religion; and *Amen!* is the best he can do towards praying.

[18] That is, the *real* or *veritable* Trinculo. The Poet often has *very* so.

[19] *Moon-calf* was an imaginary monster, supposed to be generated or misshapen through lunar influence. So in Holland's Pliny: "A false conception called *mola*, that is a moone-calfe; that is to say, a lump of flesh without shape, without life." — *Siege* is an old word for *seat.* So in *Measure for Measure,* iv. 2: "Upon the very *siege* of justice."

Trin. I took him to be kill'd with a thunder-stroke. But art thou not drown'd, Stephano? I hope, now, thou art not drown'd? Is the storm overblown? I hid me under the dead moon-calf's gaberdine for fear of the storm. And art thou living, Stephano? O Stephano, two Neapolitans 'scaped!

Steph. Pr'ythee, do not turn me about; my stomach is not constant.

Cal. [*Aside.*] These be fine things, an if[30] they be not
        sprites.
That's a brave god, and bears celestial liquor:
I will kneel to him.

Steph. How didst thou 'scape? How camest thou hither? swear, by this bottle, how thou camest hither. I escaped upon a butt of sack, which the sailors heaved o'erboard, by this bottle! which I made of the bark of a tree with mine own hands, since I was cast ashore.

Cal. I'll swear, upon that bottle, to be thy
True subject; for the liquor is not earthly.

Steph. Here; swear, man, how thou escapedst.

Trin. Swam ashore, man, like a duck: I can swim like a duck, I'll be sworn.

Steph. Here, kiss the book. [*Gives him drink.*] Though thou canst swim like a duck, thou art made like a goose.

Trin. O Stephano, hast any more of this?

Steph. The whole butt, man: my cellar is in a rock by the sea-side, where my wine is hid. — How now, moon-calf! how does thine ague?

Cal. Hast thou not dropp'd from heaven?

[30] In old English, *if, an,* and *an if* are exactly equivalent expressions; the latter being merely a reduplication; though it sometimes has the force of *even if.* See *Hamlet,* page 89, note 34.

Steph. Out o' the Moon, I do assure thee : I was the Man-i'-the-moon when time was.

Cal. I've seen thee in her, and I do adore thee :
My mistress show'd me thee, and thy dog, and thy bush.[21]

Steph. Come, swear to that ; kiss the book : I will furnish it anon with new contents : swear.   [*Gives* CALIBAN *drink.*

Trin. By this good light, this is a very shallow monster ! — I afeard of him ! — a very weak monster ! — *The Man-i'-the-moon !* — a most poor credulous monster ! — Well drawn, monster, in good sooth.[22]

Cal. I'll show thee every fertile inch o' the island ;
And I will kiss thy foot : I pr'ythee, be my god.

Trin. By this light, a most perfidious and drunken monster ! when his god's asleep, he'll rob his bottle.[23]

Cal. I'll kiss thy foot ; I'll swear myself thy subject.

Steph. Come on then ; down, and swear.

Trin. I shall laugh myself to death at this puppy-headed monster. A most scurvy monster ! I could find in my heart to beat him, —

Steph. Come, kiss.   [*Gives* CALIBAN *drink.*

Trin. — but that the poor monster's in drink : an abominable monster !

Cal. I'll show thee the best springs ; I'll pluck thee berries ;
I'll fish for thee, and get thee wood enough.
A plague upon the tyrant that I serve !
I'll bear him no more sticks, but follow thee,
Thou wondrous man.

----

[21] So in *A Midsummer-Night's Dream*, v. 1 : "This man, with lantern, dog, and bush of thorn, presenteth moonshine."

[22] *Well drawn* probably means that Caliban has taken a large *draught* of the liquor ; as we should say, a *bumper.* — " In good sooth," *sooth* is the same as *truth.* So *soothsayer* originally meant a *truth-speaker.*

[23] That is, will steal the liquor out of his bottle.

Trin. A most ridiculous monster, to make a wonder of a poor drunkard !

Cal. I pr'ythee, let me bring thee where crabs grow ;
And I with my long nails will dig thee pig-nuts ;[24]
Show thee a jay's nest, and instruct thee how
To snare the nimble marmozet ; I'll bring thee
To clustering filberts, and sometimes I'll get thee
Young staniels [25] from the rock.   Wilt thou go with me ?

Steph. I pr'ythee now, lead the way without any more talking. — Trinculo, the King and all our company else being drown'd, we will inherit here.   Here, bear my bottle : fellow Trinculo, we'll fill him by-and-by again.

Cal. [*Sings drunkenly.*]   Farewell, master ; farewell,
        farewell !

Trin. A howling monster ; a drunken monster !

Cal. No more dams I'll make for fish ;
            Nor fetch in firing at requiring ;
        Nor scrape trencher, nor wash dish :
            'Ban, 'Ban, Ca — Caliban
            Has a new master ; get a new man.

Freedom, hey-day, hey-day, freedom ! freedom, hey-day,
        freedom !

Steph. O brave monster ! lead the way.   [*Exeunt.*

[24] *Pig-nuts* are probably much the same as what we call *ground-nuts,* — a small bulbous root growing wild.
[25] The *staniel* is a species of hawk, also called kestril ; a "beautiful species," says Montagu. See Critical Notes.

ACT III.

SCENE I.—*Before* PROSPERO's *Cell.*

Enter FERDINAND, *bearing a log.*

Ferd. There be some sports are painful, and their labour
Delight in them sets off:[1] some kinds of baseness
Are nobly undergone ; and most poor matters
Point to rich ends.   This my mean task would be
As heavy to me as 'tis odious, but
The mistress which I serve quickens what's dead,
And makes my labours pleasures : O, she is
Ten times more gentle than her father's crabbed,
And he's composed of harshness.   I must remove
Some thousands of these logs, and pile them up,
Upon a sore injunction : my sweet mistress
Weeps when she sees me work ; and says such baseness
Had never like executor.   I forget :
But these sweet thoughts do even refresh my labour ;
Most busy when I do it least.[2]

[1] The delight we take in those painful sports *offsets* or *compensates* the exertion they put us to. A similar thought occurs in *Macbeth :* " The labour we delight in physics pain."

[2] That is, "*I being* most busy when I am least occupied."   The sense of the two lines appears to be, " The sweet thoughts attending my labour; and springing from what Miranda is thereby moved to say, make even the labour itself refreshing to me; so that I am happiest when I work hardest, and most weary when working least."   And Ferdinand "forgets" his task, or loses all sense of its irksomeness, in the pleasantness of his thoughts. The passage is not so very dark to those who have had their labour sweetened to them by thoughts of the dear ones for whom they were working. "And Jacob served seven years for Rachel; and they seemed unto him but a few days, for the love he had to her."   See Critical Notes.

Enter MIRANDA ; *and* PROSPERO *behind.*

Mira.   Alas, now, pray you,
Work not so hard : I would the lightning had
Burnt up those logs that you're enjoin'd to pile !
Pray, set it down, and rest you : when this burns,
'Twill weep for having wearied you.   My father
Is hard at study ; pray now, rest yourself :
He's safe for these three hours.

Ferd.   O most dear mistress,
The Sun will set before I shall discharge
What I must strive to do.

Mira.   If you'll sit down,
I'll bear your logs the while : pray, give me that ;
I'll carry't to the pile.

Ferd.   No, precious creature ;
I'd rather crack my sinews, break my back,
Than you should such dishonour undergo,
While I sit lazy by.

Mira.   It would become me
As well as it does you : and I should do it
With much more ease ; for my good will is to it,
And yours it is against.

Pros. [*Aside.*]   Poor worm, thou art infected !
This visitation shows it.

Mira.   You look wearily.

Ferd. No, noble mistress ; 'tis fresh morning with me
When you are by at night.   I do beseech you, —
Chiefly that I might set it in my prayers, —
What is your name ?

Mira.   Miranda : — O my father,
I've broke your hest to say so !

Ferd.   Admired Miranda !

Indeed the top of admiration ; worth
What's dearest to the world ! Full many a lady
I've eyed with best regard ; and many a time
The harmony of their tongues hath into bondage
Brought my too diligent ear : for several virtues
Have I liked several women ; never any
With so full soul, but some defect in her
Did quarrel with the noblest grace she owed,
And put it to the foil :[3] but you, O you,
So perfect and so peerless, are created
Of every creature's best !
  Mira.   I do not know
One of my sex ; no woman's face remember,
Save, from my glass, mine own ; nor have I seen
More that I may call men, than you, good friend,
And my dear father : how features are abroad,
I'm skilless of ; but, by my modesty, —
The jewel in my dower, — I would not wish
Any companion in the world but you ;
Nor can imagination form a shape,
Besides yourself, to like of. But I prattle
Something too wildly, and my father's precepts
I therein do forget.
  Ferd.   I am, in my condition,
A prince, Miranda ; I do think, a king, —
I would, not so ! — and would no more endure
This wooden slavery than to suffer
The flesh-fly blow[4] my mouth. Hear my soul speak :

---

[3] " Put it to the foil" means, apparently, compel it to *fight*, or to *stand on its defence ; foil* being often used as a general term for weapons of the sword kind. Here, as usual, *owed* is *owned*.

[4] The *flesh-fly* is the fly that *blows* dead flesh, that is, lays maggot-eggs upon it, and so hastens its putrefaction.

The very instant that I saw you, did
My heart fly to your service; there resides,
To make me slave to it; and for your sake
Am I this patient log-man.

    Mira.   Do you love me?

    Ferd. O Heaven, O Earth, bear witness to this sound,
And crown what I profess with kind event,
If I speak true! if hollowly, invert
What best is boded me to mischief! I,
Beyond all limit of what else[5] i' the world,
Do love, prize, honour you.

    Mira.   I am a fool
To weep at what I'm glad of.

    Pros. [*Aside.*]   Fair encounter
Of two most rare affections! Heavens rain grace
On that which breeds between them!

    Ferd.   Wherefore weep you?

    Mira. At mine unworthiness, that dare not offer
What I desire to give; and much less take
What I shall die to want.[6] But this is trifling;
And all the more it seeks to hide itself,
The bigger bulk it shows. Hence, bashful cunning!
And prompt me, plain and holy innocence!
I am your wife, if you will marry me;
If not, I'll die your maid: to be your fellow[7]
You may deny me; but I'll be your servant,

---

   [5] "*What* else" for *whatsoever* else. The Poet has many instances of relative pronouns thus used *indefinitely.* So in *King Lear,* v. 3: "*What* in the world he is that names me traitor, villain-like he lies." And in *Othello,* iii. 3: "*Who* steals my purse steals trash."

   [6] Die *from wanting,* or *by wanting.* Another gerundial infinitive. We have a like expression in *Much Ado:* "You kill me *to deny* it."

   [7] *Fellow* for *companion* or *equal,* as before. See page 89, note 50.

Whether you will or no.

    Ferd.   My mistress, dearest,

And I thus humble ever.

    Mira.   My husband, then?

    Ferd. Ay, with a heart as willing

As bondage e'er of freedom :[8] here's my hand.

    Mira. And mine, with my heart in't : and now farewell

Till half an hour hence.

    Ferd.   A thousand thousand ![9]

                [Exeunt FERDINAND *and* MIRANDA.

    Pros. So glad of this as they, I cannot be,

Who am surprised withal ;[10] but my rejoicing

At nothing can be more.   I'll to my book ;

For yet, ere supper-time, must I perform

Much business appertaining.   *[Exit.*

---

[8] The abstract for the concrete.   "I accept you for my wife as willingly as ever a bondman accepted of freedom."

[9] Meaning a thousand thousand *farewells;* this word being taken literally, like the Latin *bene vale.* — Coleridge comments on this sweet scene as follows : "The whole courting-scene, in the beginning of the third Act, is a masterpiece ; and the first dawn of disobedience in the mind of Miranda to the command of her father is very finely drawn, so as to seem the working of the Scriptural command, *Thou shalt leave father and mother,* &c.   O, with what exquisite purity this scene is conceived and executed!   Shakespeare may sometimes be gross, but I boldly say that he is always moral and modest.   Alas! in this our day, decency of manners is preserved at the expense of morality of heart, and delicacies for vice are allowed, whilst grossness against it is hypocritically, or at least morbidly, condemned."

[10] Prospero may well be surprised at what has shot up between his daughter and the Prince ; for, though the result is just what he has planned and hoped for, it has come on far better than he has dared to expect.   See Critical Notes.

SCENE II. — *Another part of the Island.*

Enter CALIBAN, STEPHANO, *and* TRINCULO, *with a bottle.*

Steph. Tell not me: when the butt is out, we will drink water; not a drop before: therefore bear up, and board 'em.[1] — Servant-monster, drink to me.

Trin. Servant-monster! the folly of this island! They say there's but five upon this isle: we are three of them; if th' other two be brain'd like us, the State totters.

Steph. Drink, servant-monster, when I bid thee: thy eyes are almost set[2] in thy head.   [CALIBAN *drinks.*

Trin. Where should they be set else? he were a brave monster indeed, if they were set in his tail.

Steph. My man-monster hath drown'd his tongue in sack: for my part, the sea cannot drown me; I swam, ere I could recover the shore, five-and-thirty leagues, off and on, by this light. — Thou shalt be my lieutenant, monster, or my standard.[3]

Trin. Your lieutenant, if you list; he's no standard.[4]

Steph. We'll not run, Monsieur Monster.

Trin. Nor go neither: but you'll lie like dogs, and yet say nothing neither.

Steph. Moon-calf, speak once in thy life, if thou be'st a good moon-calf.

---

[1] "To bear up, put the helm up, and keep a vessel off her course." So says Admiral Smith.

[2] *Set* here means, I suppose, fixed in a vacant stare. So in *Twelfth Night*, v. 1: "He's drunk, Sir Toby, an hour agone; his *eyes were set* at eight i' the morning."

[3] *Standard*, like *ensign*, is put for the *bearer* of the standard.

[4] Trinculo is punning upon *standard*, and probably means that Caliban is too drunk to *stand.*

Cal. How does thy Honour?   Let me lick thy shoe.
I'll not serve him, he is not valiant.

Trin. Thou liest, most ignorant monster: I am in case
to justle a constable.[5]   Why, thou debosh'd[6] fish, thou,
was there ever man a coward that hath drunk so much sack
as I to-day?   Wilt thou tell a monstrous lie, being but half a
fish and half a monster?

Cal. Lo, how he mocks me ! wilt thou let him, my lord?

Trin. Lord, quoth he.   That a monster should be such
a natural ![7]

Cal. Lo, lo, again ! bite him to death, I pr'ythee.

Steph. Trinculo, keep a good tongue in your head: if
you prove a mutineer, — the next tree.   The poor monster's
my subject, and he shall not suffer indignity.

Cal. I thank my noble lord.   Wilt thou be pleased
To hearken once again the suit I made thee?

Steph. Marry, will I : kneel, and repeat it ; I will stand,
and so shall Trinculo.

Enter ARIEL, *invisible.*

Cal. As I told thee before, I am subject to a tyrant ; a
sorcerer, that by his cunning hath cheated me of the island.

Ari. Thou liest.

Cal.   Thou liest, thou jesting monkey, thou :
I would my valiant master would destroy thee !
I do not lie.

---

[5] The jester is breaking jests upon himself; his meaning being, "One so
deep in drink as I am is valiant enough to quarrel with an officer of the
law."

[6] *Debosh'd* is an old form of *debauched*.   Cotgrave explains, "Deboshed,
lewd, incontinent, ungracious, dissolute, naught."

[7] *Natural* was used for *simpleton* or *fool*.   There is also a quibble intended between *monster* and *natural*, a monster being *unnatural.*

Steph. Trinculo, if you trouble him any more in's tale, by this hand, I will supplant some of your teeth.

Trin. Why, I said nothing.

Steph. Mum, then, and no more. — [*To* CAL.] Proceed.

Cal. I say, by sorcery he got this isle;
From me he got it. If thy Greatness will
Revenge it on him, — for, I know, thou darest,
But this thing dare not, —

Steph.   That's most certain.

Cal. — Thou shalt be lord of it, and I will serve thee.

Steph. How now shall this be compass'd? Canst thou bring me to the party?

Cal. Yea, yea, my lord; I'll yield him thee asleep,
Where thou mayst knock a nail into his head.

Ari. Thou liest; thou canst not.

Cal. What a pied ninny's this![8] — Thou scurvy patch! —
I do beseech thy Greatness, give him blows,
And take his bottle from him: when that's gone,
He shall drink nought but brine; for I'll not show him
Where the quick freshes[9] are.

Steph. Trinculo, run into no further danger: interrupt the monster one word further, and, by this hand, I'll turn my mercy out of doors, and make a stock-fish[10] of thee.

Trin. Why, what did I? I did nothing. I'll go further off.

Steph. Didst thou not say he lied?

Ari. Thou liest.

---

[8] *Pied* is *dappled* or *diversely-coloured.* Trinculo is " an allowed Fool" or jester, and wears a motley dress. *Patch* refers to the same circumstance.

[9] *Quick freshes* are living springs of fresh water.

[10] A *stock-fish* appears to have been a thing for practising upon with the fist, or with a cudgel. Ben Jonson has it in *Every Man in his Humour*, iii, 2: "'Slight, peace! thou wilt be beaten like a *stock-fish.*"

Steph. Do I so? take thou that. [*Strikes him.*] As you like this, give me the lie another time.

Trin. I did not give thee the lie. Out o' your wits and hearing too? A pox o' your bottle! this can sack and drinking do. A murrain on your monster, and the Devil take your fingers!

Cal. Ha, ha, ha!

Steph. Now, forward with your tale. — Pry'thee stand further off.

Cal. Beat him enough: after a little time,
I'll beat him too.

Steph. Stand further. — Come, proceed.

Cal. Why, as I told thee, 'tis a custom with him
I' the afternoon to sleep: then thou mayst brain him,[11]
Having first seized his books; or with a log
Batter his skull, or paunch him with a stake,
Or cut his weazand[12] with thy knife. Remember,
First to possess his books; for without them
He's but a sot,[13] as I am, nor hath not
One spirit to command: they all do hate him
As rootedly as I. Burn but his books.
He has brave útensils,[14] — for so he calls them, —
Which, when he has a house, he'll deck't withal:

[11] That is, knock out his brains. So, in *1 Henry the Fourth*, ii. 3, Hotspur says, "Zwounds! an I were now by this rascal, I could *brain* him with his lady's fan."

[12] *Weasand* is *windpipe* or *throat*. So Spenser has *weasand-pipe*.

[13] *Sot*, from the French, was frequently used for *fool;* as our word *besotted* sometimes is. The Poet has it repeatedly so.

[14] Here *utensils* has the accent on the first and third syllables. Such, it seems, is the English pronunciation of the word. So Wordsworth has it; and so Milton, in *Paradise Regained*, iii. 336:—

> Mules after these, camels, and dromedaries,
> And wagons, fraught with *utensils* of war.

And that most deeply to consider is
The beauty of his daughter ; he himself
Calls her a nonpareil : I ne'er saw woman,
But only Sycorax my dam and she ;
But she as far surpasseth Sycorax
As great'st does least.

    Steph.   Is it so brave a lass ?

    Cal. Ay, lord.

    Steph. Monster, I will kill this man : his daughter and I
will be king and queen, — save our Graces ! — and Trinculo
and thyself shall be viceroys. — Dost thou like the plot,
Trinculo?

    Trin. Excellent.

    Steph. Give me thy hand : I am sorry I beat thee ; but,
while thou livest, keep a good tongue in thy head.

    Cal. Within this half-hour will he be asleep :
Wilt thou destroy him then? .

    Steph. Ay, on mine honour.

    Ari. This will I tell my master.

    Cal. Thou makest me merry ; I am full of pleasure :
Let us be jocund : will you troll the catch
You taught me but while-ere ?[15]

    Steph. At thy request, monster, I will do reason,[16] any
reason. — Come on, Trunculo, let us sing.   [*Sings.*

Flout 'em and scout 'em, and scout 'em and flout 'em ;
Thought is free.

   [15] *While-ere* is *awhile since.* Milton has another form of it in the opening of *Paradise Regained :* "I who *erewhile* the happy garden sung," &c. —
A *catch* is a song in parts, where all the singers sing the same notes, but in
such order as to make harmony, and where each in turn *catches* the others ;
sometimes called a *round.* — To *troll* is to *roll* or *round out* glibly or volubly.

   [16] That is, will do what is *reasonable.* See *Hamlet*, page 58, note 13.

Cal. That's not the tune.

      [ARIEL *plays the tune on a tabor and pipe.*

Steph. What is this same?

Trin. This is the tune of our catch, play'd by the picture of Nobody.[17]

Steph. If thou be'st a man, show thyself in thy likeness : if thou be'st a devil, — take't as thou list.[18]

Trin. O, forgive me my sins !

Steph. He that dies pays all debts : I defy thee. — Mercy upon us !

Cal. Art thou afeard?

Steph. No, monster, not I.

Cal. Be not afeard ; the isle is full of noises,
Sounds and sweet airs that give delight and hurt not.
Sometime [19] a thousand twangling instruments
Will hum about mine ears ; and sometime voices,
That, if I then had waked after long sleep,
Will make me sleep again : and then, in dreaming,
The clouds methought would open, and show riches
Ready to drop upon me ; that, when I waked,
I cried to dream again.

Steph. This will prove a brave kingdom to me, where I shall have my music for nothing.

Cal. When Prospero is destroy'd.

Steph. That shall be by-and-by : I remember the story.

Cal. The sound is going away ; let's follow it,
And after do our work.

[17] *The picture of Nobody* was a common sign, and consisted of a head upon two legs, with arms. There was also a wood-cut prefixed to an old play of *Nobody and Somebody*, which represented this personage.

[18] Here Stephano probably shakes his fist at the invisible musician, or the supposed devil, by way of defiance or bravado.

[19] *Sometime*, again, for *sometimes.* See page 92, note 4.

Steph. Lead, monster; we'll follow. — I would I could see this taborer![20] he lays it on. — Wilt come?

Trin. I'll follow, Stephano.   [*Exeunt.*

SCENE III. — *Another part of the Island.*

Enter ALONSO, SEBASTIAN, ANTONIO, GONZALO, ADRIAN, FRANCISCO, *and Others.*

Gonza. By'r lakin,[1] I can go no further, sir ;
My old bones ache : here's a maze trod, indeed,
Through forth-rights and meanders ![2] by your patience,
I needs must rest me.

Alon.   Old lord, I cannot blame thee,
Who am myself attach'd with weariness,
To th' dulling of my spirits : sit down, and rest.
Even here I will put off my hope, and keep it
No longer for my flatterer : he is drown'd
Whom thus we stray to find ; and the sea mocks
Our frustrate[3] search on land.   Well, let him go.

---

[20] "You shall heare in the ayre the sound of *tabers and other instruments*, to put the travellers in feare, by evill spirites that makes these soundes, and also do call diverse of the travellers by their names." *Travels of Marcus Paulus*, 1579.   To some of these circumstances Milton also alludes in *Comus* : —

> Of calling shapes, and beckoning shadows dire :
> And aery tongues that syllable men's names
> On sands, and shores, and desert wildernesses.

[1] *By'r lakin* is a contraction of *by our ladykin*, which, again, is a diminutive of *our Lady*.   A disguised or softened form of swearing by the Blessed Virgin.

[2] *Forth-rights* are straight lines ; *meanders*, crooked ones.

[3] *Frustrate* for *frustrated*, meaning *baffled ;* in accordance with the usage remarked in note 43, page 56.   Shakespeare has many preterite forms made in the same way, such as *confiscate, consecrate, articulate,* and *suffocate.* The usage still holds in a few words, as in *situate.*

Anto. [*Aside to* SEBAS.] I am right glad that he's so out
　　of hope.
Do not, for one repulse, forgo the purpose
That you resolved t' effect.
　　Sebas. [*Aside to* ANTO.] The next advantage
Will we take throughly.[4]
　　Anto. [*Aside to* SEBAS.] Let it be to-night ·
For, now they are oppress'd with travel, they
Will not, nor cannot, use such vigilance
As when they're fresh.
　　Sebas. [*Aside to* ANTO.] I say, to-night: no more.
　　　　　　　　　　　　[*Solemn and strange music*
　　Alon. What harmony is this? My good friends, hark !
　　Gonza. Marvellous sweet music !

Enter PROSPERO *above, invisible. Enter, below, severa*
strange Shapes, bringing in a Banquet: they dance about
it with gentle actions of salutation; and, inviting the
KING, *&c., to eat, they depart.*

　　Alon. Give us kind keepers, Heavens ! — What were
　　　　these ?
　　Sebas. A living drollery.[5] Now I will believe
That there are unicorns ; that in Arabia
There is one tree, the phœnix' throne ;[6] one phœnix
At this hour reigning there.

---

　　[4] *Through* and *thorough, throughly* and *thoroughly*, are but different forms
of the same word, as to be *thorough* in a thing is to *go through* it. The old
writers use the two forms indifferently. So in St. Matthew, iii. 12: " He will
throughly purge his floor."

　　[5] Shows, called *Drolleries*, were in Shakespeare's time performed by
puppets only. " A living drollery " is therefore a drollery performed not by
puppets but by living personages ; a *live puppet-show.*

　　[6] This imaginary bird is often referred to by the old poets ; by Shakespeare repeatedly. The ancient belief is expressed by Lyly in his *Euphues,*

Anto.　　　　　　　　　　I'll believe both;
And what does else want credit, come to me,
And I'll be sworn 'tis true: travellers ne'er did lie,
Though fools at home condemn 'em.
　　Gonza.　　　　　　　　　　If in Naples
I should report this now, would they believe me?
If I should say I saw such islanders, —
For, certes,[7] these are people of the island, —
Who, though they are of monstrous shape, yet, note,
Their manners are more gentle-kind than of
Our human generation you shall find
Many, nay, almost any.
　　Pros. [*Aside.*]　　　　Honest lord,
Thou hast said well; for some of you there present
Are worse than devils.
　　Alon.　　　　　　　　I cannot too much muse[8]
Such shapes, such gesture, and such sound, expressing —
Although they want the use of tongue — a kind
Of excellent dumb discourse.
　　Pros. [*Aside.*]　　　　Praise in departing.[9]
　　Fran. They vanish'd strangely.
　　Sebas.　　　　　　　　　　No matter, since
They've left their viands behind; for we have stomachs. —
Will't please you taste of what is here?

---

thus: "For as there is but one Phœnix in the world, so there is but one tree
in Arabia, wherein she buildeth." Also in Holland's Pliny: "I myself have
heard strange things of this kind of tree; namely, in regard of the bird Phœnix; for it was assured unto me, that the said bird died with that tree, and
revived of itself as the tree sprung again."

[7] *Certes* for *certainly;* used several times by Shakespeare.

[8] To *muse* is to *wonder;* to *wonder at,* in this instance.

[9] "Praise in departing" is said to have been a proverbial phrase meaning, praise not your entertainment too soon; wait till the end.

Alon.   Not I.

Gonza. Faith, sir, you need not fear. When we were
        boys,
Who would believe that there were mountaineers
Dew-lapp'd like bulls, whose throats had hanging at 'em
Wallets of flesh?[10] or that there were such men
Whose heads stood in their breasts?[11] which now we find,
Each putter-out of one for five[12] will bring us
Good warrant of.

Alon.   I will stand to, and feed,
Although my last : no matter, since I feel
The best is past. — Brother, my lord the Duke,
Stand to, and do as we.

Thunder and lightning. Enter ARIEL, *like a harpy; claps
his wings upon the table; and, by a quaint device, the
banquet vanishes.*

Ari. You are three men of sin, whom Destiny —
That hath to[13] instrument this lower world

[10] In the Alpine and other mountainous regions are many well-known
cases of *goitre* that answer to this description. Probably, in the Poet's time,
some such had been seen by travellers, but not understood.

[11] These were probably the same that Othello speaks of: " The Anthro-
pophagi, and men whose heads do grow beneath their shoulders." Also in
Holland's Pliny: " The Blemmyi, by report, have no heads, but mouth and
eyes both in their breast."

[12] A sort of inverted life-insurance was practised by travellers in Shakespeare's time. Before going abroad they *put out* a sum of money, for which
they were to receive two, three, four, or even five times the amount upon
their return; the rate being according to the supposed danger of the expe-
dition. Of course the sum put out fell to the depositary, in case the *putter-
out* did not return. So in Ben Jonson's *Every Man out of his Humour*, ii. 1 :
" I am determined to put forth some five thousand pound, to be paid me
five for one, upon the return of myself and wife, and my dog, from the Turk's
Court in Constantinople."

[13] *To*, again, with the force of *for* or *as*. See page 78, note 9.

And what is in't — the never-surfeited sea
Hath caused to belch up ; yea, and on this island
Where man doth not inhabit ; you 'mongst men
Being most unfit to live.   I've made you mad ;
And even with such like valour men hang and drown
Their proper selves.

               [*Seeing* ALON., SEBAS., &c., *draw their swords.*

                  You fools ! I and my fellows
Are ministers of Fate : the elements,
Of whom your swords are temper'd, may as well
Wound the loud winds, or with bemock'd-at stabs
Kill the still-closing waters,[14] as diminish
One dowle[15] that's in my plume : my fellow-ministers
Are like invulnerable.   If you could hurt,
Your swords are now too massy for your strengths,
And will not be uplifted.   But remember, —
For that's my business to you, — that you three
From Milan did supplant good Prospero ;
Exposed unto the sea, which hath requit[16] it,
Him and his innocent child : for which foul deed
The powers, delaying, not forgetting, have
Incensed the seas and shores, yea, all the creatures,
Against your peace.   Thee of thy son, Alonso,
They have bereft ; and do pronounce, by me,
Lingering perdition — worse than any death
Can be at once — shall step by step attend
You and your ways ; whose wraths to guard you from, —
Which here, in this most desolate isle, else falls

[14] Waters that *continually* close over cuts made in them, and leave no
trace thereof.   See page 61, note 62.

[15] *Dowle* and *down* are said to have been equivalent.   Here *dowle* seems
rather to mean a single particle or thread of downe.

[16] *Requit* for *requited*, like others noted before.   See page 56, note 43.

Upon your heads, — is nothing, but heart-sorrow
And a clear life ensuing.[17]

*He vanishes in thunder; then, to soft music, enter the Shapes
again, and dance with mocks and mowes, and carry out
the table.*

Pros. [*Aside.*] Bravely the figure of this harpy hast thou
Perform'd, my Ariel; a grace it had, devouring:
Of my instruction hast thou nothing 'bated
In what thou hadst to say: so, with good life,
And observation strange,[18] my meaner ministers
Their several kinds have done.[19]	My high charms work,
And these mine enemies are all knit up
In their distractions: they now are in my power;
And in these fits I leave them, while I visit
Young Ferdinand, — who they suppose is drown'd, —
And his and my loved darling.	[*Exit from above.*

Gonza. I' the name of something holy, sir, why stand you
In this strange stare?
Alon.	O, it is monstrous, monstrous!
Methought the billows spoke, and told me of it;
The winds did sing it to me; and the thunder,
That deep and dreadful organ pipe, pronounced
The name of Prosper: it did bass my trespass.
Therefore my son i' the ooze is bedded; and

---

[17] " From whose wrath nothing can shield or deliver you but heart-felt
repentance and an amended life, or doing works meet for repentance."
Whose refers to *powers*, in the sixth line before.

[18] The sense appears to be, " with all the truth of life itself, and with rare
observance of the proprieties of action."

[19] To do one's *kind* is to act out one's *nature*, or act *according to* one's
nature; though in this case the nature is an assumed one, that is, a *part.*
So, in *Antony and Cleopatra*, the rustic, speaking of the asp, says, " the worm
will *do his kind*." Also in the phrase, " The cat will after *kind*."

I'll seek him deeper than e'er plummet sounded,
And with him there lie mudded.   [*Exit.*
   Sebas.   But one fiend at a time,
I'll fight their legions o'er.
   Anto.   I'll be thy second.
          [*Exeunt* SEBASTIAN *and* ANTONIO.
   Gonza. All three of them are desperate : their great guilt,
Like poison given to work a long time after,[20]
Now 'gins to bite the spirits. — I do beseech you,
That are of suppler joints, follow them swiftly,
And hinder them from what this ecstasy[21]
May now provoke them to.
   Adri.   Follow, I pray you. [*Exeunt.*

ACT IV.

SCENE I. — *Before* PROSPERO'S *Cell.*

Enter PROSPERO, FERDINAND, *and* MIRANDA.

   Pros. If I have too austerely punish'd you,
Your compensation[1] makes amends ; for I
Have given you here a thread of mine own life,[2]
Or that for which I live ; who once again
I tender to thy hand : all thy vexations

  [20] The natives of Africa have been supposed to possess the secret how to temper poisons with such art as not to operate till several years after they were administered.

  [21] Shakespeare uses *ecstasy* for any alienation of mind, a fit, or madness.

  [1] *Your compensation* is the compensation *you receive*. Shakespeare has many instances of like construction.

  [2] "Thread of mine own life" probably means about the same as " my very *heart-strings*"; strings the breaking of which spills the life.

Were but my trials of thy love, and thou
Hast strangely stood the test : here, afore Heaven,
I ratify this my rich gift.   O Ferdinand,
Do not smile at me that I boast her off,
For thou shalt find she will outstrip all praise,
And make it halt behind her.

  Ferd.   I do believe it
Against an oracle.

  Pros. Then, as my gift, and thine own acquisition
Worthily purchased, take my daughter : but,
If thou dost break her virgin-knot [3] before
All sanctimonious [4] ceremonies may
With full and holy rite be minister'd,
No sweet aspersion [5] shall the Heavens let fall
To make this contract grow ; but barren hate,
Sour-eyed disdain, and discord, shall bestrew
The union of your bed with weeds so loathly,[6]
That you shall hate it both : therefore take heed,
As Hymen's lamps shall light you.

  Ferd.   As I hope
For quiet days, fair issue, and long life,
With such love as 'tis now, the murkiest even,
The most opportune place, the strong'st suggestion [7]
Our worser genius [8] can, shall never melt

 [3] Alluding, no doubt, to the zone or sacred girdle which the old Romans used as the symbol and safeguard of maiden honour.

 [4] *Sanctimonious*, here, is *sacred* or *religious*. The marriage *ritual* was supposed to have something of consecrating virtue in it.

 [5] *Aspersion* in its primitive sense of *sprinkling*, as with genial rain or dew. — Here, again, as also just after, *shall* for *will*.

 [6] Not with wholesome flowers, such as the bridal bed was wont to be decked with, but with *loathsome* weeds.

 [7] *Suggestion*, again, for *temptation*. See page 89, note 53.

 [8] *Genius, spirit*, and *angel* were used indifferently for what we should

Mine honour into lust; to take away
The edge of that day's celebration,
When I shall think, or Phœbus' steeds are founder'd,
Or Night kept chain'd below.

 Pros.   Fairly spoke.
Sit, then, and talk with her; she is thine own. —
What, Ariel! my industrious servant, Ariel!

      Enter ARIEL.

 Ari. What would my potent master? here I am.
 Pros. Thou and thy meaner fellows your last service
Did worthily perform; and I must use you
In such another trick. Go bring the rabble,
O'er whom I give thee power, here, to this place:
Incite them to quick motion; for I must
Bestow upon the eyes of this young couple
Some vanity [9] of mine art: it is my promise,
And they expect it from me.
 Ari.   Presently?
 Pros. Ay, with a twink.
 Ari. Before you can say *Come* and *Go,*
   And breathe twice, and cry *So, so,*
   Each one, tripping on his toe,
   Will be here with mop and mow.[10]
   Do you love me, master? — no?

call a man's worser or better *self. The Edinburgh Review,* July, 1869, has
the following: " In mediæval theology, the rational soul is an angel, the low-
est in the hierarchy for being clothed for a time in the perishing vesture of
the body. But it is not necessarily an angel of light. It may be a good or
evil genius, a guardian angel or a fallen spirit, a demon of light or darkness." See, also, *Julius Cæsar,* page 76, note 16.
 [9] Perhaps meaning some magical show or illusion. *Display?*
 [10] *Mop* and *mow* were very often used thus together. To *mow* is to *make
mouths,* to *grimace.* Wedgwood, in his *English Etymology,* says that *mop*

Pros. Dearly, my delicate Ariel. Do not approach
Till thou dost hear me call.

    Ari.   Well, I conceive.   [*Exit.*

    Pros. Look thou be true ; do not give dalliance
Too much the rein : the strongest oaths are straw
To th' fire i' the blood.

    Ferd.   I warrant you, sir :
The white-cold virgin snow upon my heart
Abates the ardour of my liver.[11]

    Pros.   Well. —
Now come, my Ariel ! bring a corollary,[12]
Rather than want a spirit : appear, and pertly !
No tongue ; all eyes ; be silent.   [*Soft music.*

Enter IRIS.

    Iris. Ceres, most bounteous lady, thy rich leas
Of wheat, rye, barley, vetches, oats, and peas ;
Thy turfy mountains, where live nibbling sheep,
And flat meads thatch'd with stover,[13] them to keep ;
Thy banks with peonéd and twillèd brims,[14]

---

has exactly the same derivation as *mock*, and means to *gibber*. Thus the
ape both *mops* and *mows* ; that is, he *gibbers* or *chatters*, and *makes faces*.

[11] The *liver* was supposed to be the special seat of certain passions, and
so was often put for the passions themselves.

[12] *Corollary* here means a surplus number ; more than enough. — *Pertly*,
in the next line, is *nimbly, alertly*.

[13] *Stover* is fodder and provision of all sorts for cattle. Steevens says
that in some counties it " signifies hay made of coarse rank grass, such as
even cows will not eat while it is green."

[14] A writer in *The Edinburgh Review* for October, 1872, argues, and, I
think, proves, that *peonéd* here refers to the *marsh-marigold*, which grew
abundantly on the flat marshy banks of such still-running streams as the
Warwickshire Avon, and which was provincially called *peony* or *piony*. He
thus compares it with the garden peony : " The flowers, though differing in
colour, have a remarkable similarity in general growth and shape, especially

Which spongy April at thy hest betrims,
To make cold nymphs chaste crowns ; and thy brown groves,
Whose shadow the dismissèd bachelor loves,
Being lass-lorn ; thy pole-clipt vineyard ; [15]
And thy sea-marge, steril, and rocky-hard,
Where thou thyself dost air ; — the Queen o' the Sky,
Whose watery arch and messenger am I,
Bids thee leave these, and with her sovereign Grace,
Here on this grass-plot, in this very place,
To come and sport.   Her peacocks fly amain :
Approach, rich Ceres, her to entertain.

Enter CERES.

Cer. Hail, many-colour'd messenger, that ne'er
Dost disobey the wife of Jupiter ;
Who, with thy saffron wings, upon my flowers
Diffusest honey-drops, refreshing showers ;
And with each end of thy blue bow dost crown
My bosky acres [16] and my unshrubb'd down,

in the early stage, when the fully-formed bud is ripe for blowing." — In explanation of *twillèd* the same writer has the following : " *Twills* is given by Halliwell as an older provincial word for *reeds;* and it was applied, like *quills*, to the serried rustling sedges of river reaches and marshy levels. It was indeed while watching the masses of waving sedge cutting the water-line of the Avon, not far from Stratford church, that we first felt the peculiar force and significance of the epithet." — In the next line, April has the epithet *spongy*, probably because at that season the earth or the air *sponges* up so much water. So, in *Cymbeline*, iv. 2, we have " the *spongy* south," referring to the south or south-west *wind*, which, in England, is apt to be densely charged with moisture ; that is, *foggy ;* elsewhere called " the foggy south."

[15] *Lass-lorn* is *forsaken by his lass*, the sweet-heart that has *dismissed* him. — *Pole-clipt* probably means poles embraced or clasped by the vines. *Clip* was often used for *embrace*. So in *Coriolanus*, i. 6: " Let me *clip* ye in arms as sound as when I woo'd." — *Vineyard* is here a trisyllable.

[16] " *Bosky* acres " are *woody* acres, fields intersected by luxuriant hedgerows and copses. So in Milton's *Comus :* —

Rich scarf to my proud Earth ; — why hath thy Queen
Summon'd me hither, to this short-grass'd green?

   Iris. A contract of true love to celebrate ;
And some donation freely to estate
On the bless'd lovers.

   Cer.   Tell me, heavenly Bow,
If Venus or her son, as thou dost know,
Do now attend the Queen? Since they did plot
The means that dusky Dis my daughter got,[17]
Her and her blind boy's scandal'd company
I have forsworn.

   Iris.   Of her society
Be not afraid :· I met her deity
Cutting the clouds towards Paphos,[18] and her son
Dove-drawn with her. Here thought they to have done
Some wanton charm upon this man and maid,
Whose vows are, that no bed-right shall be paid
Till Hymen's torch be lighted : but in vain ;
Mars's hot minion is return'd again ;[19]
Her waspish-headed son has broke his arrows,
Swears he will shoot no more, but play with sparrows,
And be a boy right out.

> I know each lane, and every alley green,
> Dingle, or bushy dell of this wild wood,
> And every *bosky* bourn from side to side.

[17] The means whereby Pluto caught and carried off Proserpina. Proserpina was the daughter of Jupiter and Ceres : Dis, King of *dusky* Hades, fell so deep in love with her, that he must needs seize her, *vi et armis*, and spirit her away to Hades, to be his Queen.

[18] A city in Cyprus, where Venus had a favourite country-seat.

[19] Has gone back to Paphos. *Minion* is *darling* or *favourite*, and refers to *Venus.* — In what follows the meaning is, that Cupid is so chagrined and mortified at being thus baffled, that he is determined to give up his business, and act the love-god no more, but be a mere boy, or a boy *outright.*

Cer.   High'st Queen of state,[20]
Great Juno comes; I know her by her gait.[21]

Enter JUNO.

Juno. How does my bounteous sister? Go with me
To bless this twain, that they may prosperous be,
And honour'd in their issue.

SONG.

Juno.   *Honour, riches, marriage-blessing,*
            Long continuance, and increasing,
            Hourly joys be still upon you !
            Juno sings her blessings on you.

Cer.   *Earth's increase, and foison plenty,[22]*
            Barns and garners never empty ;
            Vines with clustering bunches growing ;
            Plants with goodly burden bowing ;
            Spring come to you at the farthest
            In the very end of harvest ! [23]
            Scarcity and want shall shun you ;
            Ceres' blessing so is on you.

[20] "High'st Queen of state" is the same as Queen of highest state, or
Queen above all other queens. *State* for *throne*, or *chair* of state. So the
word was often used. — The Poet has many similar inversions.

[21] Juno was distinguished by her *walk*, as the gods and goddesses generally were. So in *Pericles*, v. 1: "In *pace* another Juno."

[22] "*Foison plenty*" is, strictly speaking, redundant or tautological, as both
words mean the same. But *plenty* is used as an adjective,—*plentiful* or
overflowing. See page 82, note 24.

[23] "May your new Spring come, at the latest, as soon as the harvest of
the old one is over!" This explanation is sustained, as Staunton points
out, by Amos, ix. 13: "Behold, the days come, saith the Lord, that the
ploughman shall overtake the reaper, and the treader of grapes him that
soweth the seed." Also, in *The Faerie Queen*, iii. 6, 42: —

> There is continuall Spring, and harvest there
> Continuall, both meeting in one time.

Ferd. This is a most majestic vision, and
Harmonious charmingly.[24]   May I be bold
To think these spirits?
   Pros.   Spirits, which by mine art
I have from their confines call'd to enact
My present fancies.
   Ferd.   Let me live here ever;
So rare a wonder'd [25] father and a wife
Make this place Paradise.   [JUNO *and* CERES *whisper, and*
                                  send IRIS *on employment.*
   Pros.   Sweet, now, silence!
Juno and Ceres whisper seriously;
There's something else to do: hush, and be mute,
Or else our spell is marr'd.[26]
   Iris. You nymphs, call'd Naiads, of the winding brooks,
With your sedge crowns and ever-harmless looks,
Leave your crisp channels,[27] and on this green land

---

[24] That is, charmingly harmonious. See note 20, above.—"*So* bold *as*
to think." See page 54, note 28.

[25] "So rare-wonder'd a father" is the prose order of the words. The
Poet has several such inversions for metre's sake. So in *King John*, iv. 1:
"For putting on so new a fashion'd robe." So new-fashion'd a robe. The
meaning in the text is, so *rarely-wonderful* a father; and the force of "so rare
a *wonder'd*" extends over *wife*. Shakespeare has many instances of the
ending -*ed* used in the same way; as in *Macbeth*, iii. 4: "You have broke
the good meeting with most *admired* disorder." *Admired* for *admirable*,
and in the sense of *wonderful*.

[26] It was supposed that any noise or disturbance would upset or discon-
cert "the might of magic spells."

[27] *Crisp* is *curled*, from the curl made by a breeze on the surface of the
water. The transference of an epithet to an associated object, as of *crisp*
from the water to the channel in this instance, is one of Shakespeare's favourite traits of style. So in *Romeo and Juliet*, iii. 5, when the lovers see
tokens of the dawn that is to *sever* them, Romeo says, "what envious streaks
do lace the *severing clouds* in yonder east."

Answer our summons ; Juno does command :
Come, temperate nymphs, and help to celebrate
A contract of true love ; be not too late. —

Enter certain Nymphs.

You sun-burn'd sicklemen, of August weary,
Come hither from the furrow, and be merry :
Make holiday ; your rye-straw hats put on,
And these fresh nymphs encounter every one
In country footing.

Enter certain Reapers, *properly habited : they join with the*
Nymphs in a graceful dance; towards the end whereof
PROSPERO *starts suddenly, and speaks; after which, to*
a strange, hollow, and confused noise, they heavily vanish.

Pros. [*Aside.*] I had forgot that foul conspiracy
Of the beast Caliban and his confederates
Against my life : the minute of their plot
Is almost come. — [*To the* Spirits.] Well done ; avoid ;[28]
    no more !
Ferd. This is most strange : your father's in some passion
That works him strongly.
Mira.   Never till this day
Saw I him touch'd with anger so distemper'd.
Pros. You do, my son, look in a movèd sort,[29]
As if you were dismay'd : be cheerful, sir.
Our revels now are ended.   These our actors,
As I foretold you, were all spirits, and
Are melted into air, into thin air :
And, like the baseless fabric of this vision,

[28] *Vacate* or *make void* the place; that is to say, *be gone.*

[29] Here, as often, *sort* is *manner* or *way.* So in *Coriolanus*, i. 3 : " I pray
you, daughter, express yourself in a more comfortable *sort*."

The cloud-capp'd towers, the gorgeous palaces,
The solemn temples, the great globe itself,
Yea, all which it inherit,[30] shall dissolve,
And, like this insubstantial pageant faded,[31]
Leave not a rack[32] behind. We are such stuff
As dreams are made on, and our little life
Is rounded with a sleep.[33] Sir, I am vex'd ;
Bear with my weakness ; my old brain is troubled :
Be not disturb'd with my infirmity :
If you be pleased, retire into my cell,
And there repose : a turn or two I'll walk,
To still my beating mind.

Ferd. ⎱
Mira. ⎰   We wish you peace.

Pros. [*To* ARIEL.] Come with a thought ! — I thank
ye.[34] [*Exeunt* FERD. *and* MIRA:] — Ariel, come !

Re-enter ARIEL.

Ari. Thy thoughts I cleave to : what's thy pleasure ?
Pros.   Spirit,
We must prepare to meet with[35] Caliban.

[30] All who *possess* it. Such is often the meaning of *inherit*. So in the divine beatitude, "Blessed are the meek; for they shall *inherit* the earth."

[31] *Faded*, from the Latin *vado*, is the same as *vanished*.

[32] *Rack* was used of the highest, and therefore lightest or thinnest clouds. So in Bacon's *Silva Silvarum :* "The winds in the upper region (which move the *clouds* above, which we call the *rack*, and are not perceived below) pass without noise." See, also, *Hamlet*, page 118, note 77.— The word *rack* is from *reek*, that is, *vapour* or *smoke*. See Critical Notes.

[33] *On* for *of*. Still used so, especially in colloquial speech. — *Rounded* is *finished, rounded off*. The sleep here meant is the sleep of death ; as in Hamlet's soliloquy : " To die, to sleep ; no more."

[34] " I thank ye" is addressed to Ferdinand and Miranda, in return for their " We wish you peace."

[35] *To meet with* was anciently the same as to *counteract* or *oppose*. So in

Ari. Ay, my commander : when I presented Ceres,
I thought t' have told thee of it ; but I fear'd
Lest I might anger thee.

Pros. Well, say again, where didst thou leave these varlets ?

Ari. I told you, sir, they were red-hot with drinking ;
So full of valour, that they smote the air
For breathing in their faces ; beat the ground
For kissing of their feet ; yet always bending
Towards their project.   Then I beat my tabor ;
At which, like unback'd colts, they prick'd their ears,
Advanced [36] their eyelids, lifted up their noses
As they smelt music : so I charm'd their ears,
That, calf-like, they my lowing follow'd through
Tooth'd briers, sharp furzes, pricking goss, and thorns,
Which enter'd their frail shins : at last I left them
I' the filthy-mantled pool [37] beyond your cell,
There dancing up to th' chins, that the foul lake
O'erstunk their feet. [38]

Pros.   This was well done, my bird.
Thy shape invisible retain thou still :
The trumpery in my house, go bring it hither,
For stale [39] to catch these thieves.

Herbert's *Country Parson :* " He knows the temper and pulse of every one
in his house, and accordingly either *meets with* their vices, or advanceth
their virtues."

[36] *Advanced* is *raised*, as already explained. See page 70, note 93. — In
the next line, " As they smelt," as *if* they smelt.

[37] The pool mantled with filth. *Mantle* for the scum that forms on the
surface of stagnant water. So in *The Merchant,* i. 1 : " There are a sort of
men whose visages do cream and *mantle* like a standing pond."

[38] *That* for *so that* or *insomuch that.* — The meaning of this unsavoury
passage is, that " the foul lake " was so stirred up by their dancing as to give
out a worse odour than the men's feet did before they got into it.

[39] *Stale,* in the art of fowling, signified a *bait* or *lure* to decoy birds.

Ari. I go, I go. [*Exit.*

Pros. A devil, a born devil, on whose nature
Nurture can never stick ;[40] on whom my pains,
Humanely taken, all are lost, quite lost ;
And as with age his body uglier grows,
So his mind cankers.[41] I will plague them all,
Even to roaring. —

Re-enter ARIEL *loaden with glistering apparel, &c.*

Come, hang them on this line.[42]

PROSPERO *and* ARIEL *remain, invisible. Enter* CALIBAN,
STEPHANO, *and* TRINCULO, *all wet.*

Cal. Pray you, tread softly, that the blind mole may not
Hear a foot fall : we now are near his cell.

[40] *Nurture* for *education, training,* or *culture.*

[41] As before observed, page 71, note 96, *canker* was used of an eating, malignant sore, like *cancer,* which is but another form of the same word ; and also of *rust.* I am not quite certain which of these senses it bears here ; probably the first. Shakespeare has the word repeatedly in both senses ; as in *Romeo and Juliet,* i. 1, where the first *canker'd* means *rusted,* while the second has the sense of *cancer :—*

> To wield old partisans, in hands as old,
> Canker'd with peace, to part your *canker'd* hate.

[42] Some question has been made as to what *line* means here. The word is commonly taken as meaning a *clothes-line;* but I rather agree with the late Rev. Joseph Hunter, and with Mr. A. E. Brae, that it means a *line-tree,* which may well be supposed to be growing in the lawn before Prospero's cell,—the same that Stephano addresses a little after as " Mistress Line." For Prospero is still in the same place where he has just been making a display of his art; and I can hardly think he has a clothes-line stretched across it. It has indeed been objected that *line,* meaning the line-tree, would not be used thus, without the adjunct *tree* or *grove;* but Mr. Brae disposes of this objection fairly, by quoting the following from Holinshed : " We are not without the plane, the ugh, the sorfe, the chestnut, the *line,* the black cherrie, and such like."

Steph. Monster, your fairy, which you say is a harmless fairy, has done little better than play'd the Jack with us.[43]

Trin. Monster, I do smell all horse-stale; at which my nose is in great indignation.

Steph. So is mine. — Do you hear, monster? If I should take a displeasure against you, look you, —

Trin. Thou wert but a lost monster.

Cal. Nay, good my lord,[44] give me thy favour still.
Be patient, for the prize I'll bring thee to
Shall hoodwink this mischance:[45] therefore speak softly;
All's hush'd as midnight yet.

Trin. Ay, but to lose our bottles in the pool, —

Steph. There is not only disgrace and dishonour in that, monster, but an infinite loss.

Trin. That's more to me than my wetting: yet this is your harmless fairy, monster.

Steph. I will fetch off my bottle, though I be o'er ears for my labour.

Cal. Pr'ythee, my King, be quiet. See'st thou here?
This is the mouth o' the cell: no noise, and enter.
Do that good mischief which may make this island
Thine own for ever, and I, thy Caliban,
For aye thy foot-licker.

Steph. Give me thy hand. I do begin to have bloody thoughts.

[43] To play the *Jack* is to play the *Knave;* or it may be to play the *Jack-o'-lantern,* by leading them astray.

[44] We should say "my good lord." Similar inverted phrases occur continually in old plays; such as "dread my lord," "gracious my lord," "dear my mother," "sweet my sister," "gentle my brother," &c.

[45] To *hoodwink* a thing is, apparently, to make one *overlook* it or *forget* it, to *blind* him to it, or put it out of his sight. So *hoodman-blind* is an old term for what we call blind-man's-buff.

Trin. O King Stephano! O peer!⁴⁶ O worthy Stephano! look what a wardrobe here is for thee!

Cal. Let it alone, thou fool; it is but trash. ·

Trin. O, ho, monster! we know what belongs to a frip-
pery.⁴⁷ — O King Stephano!

Steph. Put off that gown, Trinculo; by this hand, I'll
have that gown.

Trin. Thy Grace shall have it.

Cal. The dropsy drown this fool! — what do you mean,
To dote thus on such luggage? Let's along,
And do the murder first: if he awake,
From toe to crown he'll fill our skins with pinches;
Make us strange stuff.

Steph. Be you quiet, monster. — Mistress line, is not this
my jerkin? Now is the jerkin under the line: now, jerkin,
you are like to lose your hair, and prove a bald jerkin.⁴⁸

Trin. Do, do: we steal by line and level,⁴⁹ an't like your
Grace.

⁴⁶ A humorous allusion to the old ballad entitled "Take thy old Cloak
about thee," a part of which is sung by Iago in *Othello*, ii. 3. I add one
stanza of it: —

> *King Stephen was a worthy peer,*
> *His breeches cost him but a crown;*
> *He held them sixpence all too dear,*
> *Therefore he call'd the tailor lown.*

⁴⁷ *Frippery* was the name of a shop where old clothes were sold.

⁴⁸ King Stephano puns rather swiftly here. The name of the tree, as
explained in note 42, suggests to him the *equinoctial line*, under which, certain regions were much noted for their aptness to generate diseases that
commonly made the sufferers *bald*. *Jerkin* was the name of a man's upper
garment. Mr. Brae thinks there may be another quibble intended between
hair and *air*, as clothes are hung out to be *aired*, and the jerkin was likely
to lose the benefit of such *airing;* but I should rather take *hair* as referring
to the *nap* of the jerkin, which was likely to be worn off in Stephano's using;
so as to make the jerkin a *bald* jerkin in the nearer sense of having lost its *hair*.

⁴⁹ *Do, do*, is said, apparently, in commendation of Stephano's wit as dis-

Steph. I thank thee for that jest; here's a garment for't: wit shall not go unrewarded while I am king of this country. *Steal by line and level* is an excellent pass of pate;[50] there's another garment for't.

Trin. Monster, come, put some lime[51] upon your fingers, and away with the rest.

Cal. I will have none on't: we shall lose our time, And all be turn'd to barnacles,[52] or to apes With foreheads villainous low.[53]

Steph. Monster, lay-to your fingers: help to bear this away,

played in his address to the jerkin. — "Steal by *line* and level" is a further punning on the same word; the plumb-line and the level being instruments used by architects and builders. So that to steal by line and level was to *show wit* in stealing, or to steal *artistically*.

[50] *Pass of pate* is a *spurt* or *sally of wit; pass* being, in the language of fencing, a *thrust.*

[51] *Lime*, or *bird-lime*, was a sticky substance used for catching birds. So in *2 Henry the Sixth*, i. 3: "Myself have *limed* a bush for her, and placed a quire of such enticing birds, that she will light to listen to their lays." See, also, *Hamlet*, page 154, note 8.

[52] Caliban's barnacle is the *clakis* or *tree-goose*, as it was called, which was thought to be produced from the shell-fish, *lepas antifera*, also called barnacle. Gerard's *Herbal* has the following account of the matter: "There are in the north parts of Scotland certain trees whereon do grow shell-fishes, which, falling into the water, do become fowls, whom we call *barnakles*, in the north of England *brant-geese*, and in Lancashire *tree-geese*." Perhaps the old notion of the barnacle-goose being produced by the barnacle-fish grew from the identity of name. As Caliban prides himself on his intellectuality, he naturally has a horror of being turned into any thing so stupid as a goose.

[53] A low forehead was held a deformity. On the other hand, a forehead high and broad was deemed a handsome feature in man or woman. The Poet has several allusions to this old idea. So in *The Two Gentlemen*, iv. 4: "Ay, but her forehead's low, and mine's as high." And in Spenser's description of Belphœbe, *Faerie Queene*, ii. 3, 24: —

Her ivorie forehead, full of bountie brave,
Like a broad table did itselfe dispred.

where my hogshead of wine is, or I'll turn you out of my
kingdom : go to,[54] carry this.

Trin. And this.

Steph. Ay, and this.

A noise of hunters heard. Enter divers Spirits *in shape of
hounds, and hunt them about;* PROSPERO *and* ARIEL *setting them on.*

Pros. Hey, Mountain, hey !

Ari. Silver ! there it goes, Silver !

Pros. Fury, Fury ! there, Tyrant, there ! hark ! hark ! —

          [CAL., STEPH., *and* TRIN. *are driven out.*

Go charge my goblins that they grind their joints
With dry convulsions ;[55] shorten up their sinews
With agèd cramps ;[56] and more pinch-spotted make them
Than pard or cat-o'-mountain.[57]

Ari.   Hark, they roar !

Pros. Let them be hunted soundly. At this hour
Lie at my mercy all mine enemies :
Shortly shall all my labours end, and thou
Shalt have the air at freedom : for a little
Follow, and do me service.   *[Exeunt.*

[54] *Go to* is a phrase occurring very often, and of varying import, sometimes of impatience, sometimes of reproof, sometimes of encouragement.
Hush up, come on, be off, are among its meanings.

[55] In certain fevers, the mucilage sometimes gets dried out of the joints,
especially the knee-joints, so as to cause a creaking or grating sound when
the patient walks. Of course the effect is very painful.

[56] *Agèd* seems to be used here with the sense of the intensive *old,* as
before explained. See page 68, note 86.

[57] *Pard* was in common use for *leopard,* as also for *panther.* — *Cat-o'-
mountain* is probably the *wild-cat.* So in Minsheu's *Spanish Dictionary:*
" Gato montes : A cat of mountaine, a wilde cat." This animal, however,
can hardly be called *spotted;* it is rather striped. Perhaps the term was
not confined to one species of animal.

ACT V.

SCENE I. — *Before the Cell of* PROSPERO.

Enter PROSPERO *in his magic robes, and* ARIEL.

Pros. Now does my project gather to a head :
My charms crack not ; my spirits obey ; and Time
Goes upright with his carriage.[1]   How's the day?
Ari. On the sixth hour ; at which time, my lord,
You said our work should cease.
   Pros.   I did say so,
When first I raised the tempest.   Say, my spirit,
How fares the King and's followers?
   Ari.   Confined together
In the same fashion as you gave in charge ;
Just as you left them ; all are prisoners, sir,
In the line-grove which weather-fends your cell ;[2]
They cannot budge till your release.[3]   The King,
His brother, and yours, abide all three distracted ;
And the remainder mourning over them,
Brimful of sorrow and dismay ; but chiefly
He that you term'd *The good old lord, Gonzalo* :
His tears run down his beard, like winter-drops
From eaves of reeds.   Your charm so strongly works 'em,

[1] Time does not break down or bend under its load, or what it carries; that is, "we have time enough for what we have undertaken to do."
[2] "Which *defends* your cell against the weather, or the storm."
[3] "Till you release them," of course.   The objective genitive, as it is called, where present usage admits only of the subjective genitive.   The Poet has many such constructions.   See page 116, note 1.

That, if you now beheld them, your affections
Would become tender.

    Pros.   Dost thou think so, spirit?

    Ari. Mine would, sir, were I human.

    Pros.   And mine shall.

Hast thou, which art but air, a touch, a feeling
Of their afflictions, and shall not myself,
One of their kind, that relish all as sharply
Passion as they,[4] be kindlier moved than thou art?
Though with their high wrongs I am struck to th' quick,
Yet with my nobler reason 'gainst my fury
Do I take part : the rarer action is
In virtue than in vengeance : they being penitent,
The sole drift of my purpose doth extend
Not a frown further.   Go release them, Ariel :
My charms I'll break, their senses I'll restore,
And they shall be themselves.

    Ari.   I'll fetch them, sir.   [*Exit.*

    Pros. Ye elves of hills, brooks, standing lakes, and groves ;[5]
And ye that on the sands with printless foot
Do chase the ebbing Neptune, and do fly him
When he comes back ; you demi-puppets that
By moonshine do the green-sour ringlets[6] make,

---

[4] *All* is here used adverbially, in the sense of *quite;* and *passion* is the
object of *relish,* and has the sense of *suffering.*   The sense of the passage is
sometimes defeated by setting a comma after *sharply.*

[5] This speech is in some measure borrowed from Medea's, in Ovid; the
expressions are, many of them, in the old translation by Golding.   But the
exquisite fairy imagery is Shakespeare's own.

[6] These *ringlets* were circles of bright-green grass, supposed to be produced by the footsteps of fairies dancing in a ring.   The origin of them is
still, I believe, a mystery.   Alluded to in *A Midsummer-Night's Dream,* ii. 1.
— *Mushrooms* were also thought to be the work of fairies; probably from
their growing in rings, and springing up with such magical quickness.

Whereof the ewe not bites ; and you whose pastime
Is to make midnight mushrooms ; that rejoice
To hear the solemn curfew ;[7] by whose aid —
Weak masters though ye be[8] — I have be-dimm'd
The noon-tide Sun, call'd forth the mutinous winds,
And 'twixt the green sea and the azure vault
Set roaring war : to the dread-rattling thunder
Have I given fire, and rifted Jove's stout oak
With his own bolt : the strong-based promontory
Have I made shake, and by the spurs[9] pluck'd up
The pine and cedar : graves at my command
Have waked their sleepers, oped, and let 'em forth
By my so potent art.   But this rough magic
I here abjure ; and, when I have required
Some heavenly music, — which even now I do, —
To work mine end upon their senses that
This airy charm is for, I'll break my staff,
Bury it certain fathoms in the earth,
And deeper than did ever plummet sound
I'll drown my book.   [*Solemn music.*

Re-enter ARIEL : *after him,* ALONSO, *with a frantic gesture,*
    attended by GONZALO ; SEBASTIAN *and* ANTONIO *in like*
    manner, attended by ADRIAN *and* FRANCISCO : *they all*
    enter the circle which PROSPERO *had made, and there*
    stand charmed ; which PROSPERO *observing, speaks.*

[7] They rejoice, because "the curfew tolls the knell of parting day," and so signals the time for the fairies to begin their nocturnal frolics.

[8] *Weak*, if left to themselves, because they waste their force in sports and in frivolous or discordant aims ; but powerful when guided by wisdom, and trained to worthy ends. This passage has often seemed to me a strange prognostic of what human intelligence has since done in taming and marshalling the great forces of Nature into the service of man.

[9] The *spurs* are the largest and longest roots of trees.

A solemn air, as the best comforter
To an unsettled fancy, cure the brains,
Now useless, boil'd [10] within the skull ! — There stand,
For you are spell-stopp'd. —
Holy [11] Gonzalo, honourable man,
Mine eyes, even sociable to [12] the show of thine,
Fall fellowly drops. — The charm dissolves apace ;
And as the morning steals upon the night,
Melting the darkness, so their rising senses [13]
Begin to chase the ignorant fumes that mantle
Their clearer reason. — O thou good Gonzalo,
My true preserver, and a loyal sir
To him thou follow'st ! I will pay thy graces
Home [14] both in word and deed. — Most cruelly

[10] *Boil'd* for *boiling;* the passive form with the *neuter* sense: for the verb to *boil* is used as active, passive, or neuter, indifferently. We have *boil'a* just so again in *The Winter's Tale,* iii. 3: "Would any but these *boil'd* brains of nineteen and two-and-twenty hunt this weather?" — Love, madness, and melancholy are imaged by Shakespeare under the figure of *boiled* brains, or *boiling* brains, or *seething* brains. So in *A Midsummer-Night's Dream,* v. 1: "Lovers and madmen have such *seething* brains," &c. Also in *Twelfth Night,* ii. 5: "If I lose a scruple of this sport, let me be *boiled* to death with melancholy." Probably the expression grew from the heat or fever that was understood or supposed to agitate the brain in such cases.

[11] In Shakespeare's time, *holy,* besides the religious sense of *godly* or *sanctified,* was also used in the moral sense of *righteous* or *just.* And why not ?

[12] *Sociable to* is the same as *sympathetic with. — Fall,* in the next line, is evidently a transitive verb, equivalent to *let fall.* The usage was common. So in ii. 1, of this play: "To fall it on Gonzalo."

[13] *Senses* was very often used thus of the mental faculties ; as we still say of one who does not see things as they are, that he is *out of his senses.* The meaning of the passage may be given something thus: "As morning dispels the darkness, so their returning reason begins to dispel the blinding mists or fumes that are gathered about it."

[14] *Home* was much used as a strong intensive ; meaning *thoroughly,* or *to the utmost.* See *Hamlet,* page 152, note 2; and *Macbeth,* page 60, note 26.

Didst thou, Alonso, use me and my daughter:
Thy brother was a furtherer in the act;—
Thou'rt pinch'd for't now, Sebastian.— Flesh and blood,
You, brother mine, that entertain'd ambition,
Expell'd remorse and nature; [15] who, with Sebastian,—
Whose inward pinches therefore are most strong,—
Would here have kill'd your King; I do forgive thee,
Unnatural though thou art.— Their understanding
Begins to swell; and the approaching tide
Will shortly fill the reasonable shore, [16]
That now lies foul and muddy.   Not one of them
That yet looks on me, or would know me.— Ariel,
Fetch me the hat and rapier in my cell:—   [*Exit* ARIEL.
I will discase me, [17] and myself present
As I was sometime Milan:—quickly, spirit;
Thou shalt ere long be free.

   ARIEL *re-enters, singing, and helps to attire* PROSPERO.

   Ari. Where the bee sucks, there suck I:
      In a cowslip's bell I lie,—
      There I couch: when owls do cry,
      On the bat's back I do fly
      After Summer, merrily. [18]
     Merrily, merrily shall I live now
     Under the blossom that hangs on the bough.

[15] Here, as commonly in Shakespeare, *remorse* is *pity* or *tenderness of heart*. *Nature* is put for *natural affection*. Often so.

[16] "The *reasonable* shore" is the shore *of reason*.

[17] "Will put off my disguise." The Poet repeatedly uses *case* for clothes; also for *skin.— Sometime*, in the next line, is *formerly*. Often so.

[18] Ariel uses "the bat's back" as his pleasant vehicle, to pursue Summer in its progress to other regions, and thus live merrily under continual blossoms. Such appears the most natural as well as most poetical meaning

Pros. Why, that's my dainty Ariel! I shall miss thee;
But yet thou shalt have freedom : — so, so, so.
To the King's ship, invisible as thou art :
There shalt thou find the mariners asleep
Under the hatches ; the master and the boatswain
Being awaked, enforce them to this place,
And presently, I pr'ythee.

Ari. I drink the air before me, and return
Or e'er your pulse twice beat.   [*Exit* ARIEL.

Gonza. All torment, trouble, wonder, and amazement
Inhabit here : some heavenly power guide us
Out of this fearful country !

Pros.   Behold, sir King,
The wrongèd Duke of Milan, Prospero :
For more assurance that a living prince
Does now speak to thee, I embrace thy body;
And to thee and thy company I bid
A hearty welcome.

Alon.   Whêr [19] thou be'st he or no,
Or some enchanted trifle [20] to abuse me,
As late I have been, I not know : thy pulse

of this much disputed passage. As a matter of fact, however, bats do
not migrate in quest of Summer, but become torpid in winter. Was the
Poet ignorant of this, or did he disregard it, thinking that such beings as
Ariel were not bound to observe the rules of natural history? See Critical
Notes.

[19] The Poet often so contracts *whether.* See *Julius Cæsar*, page 43,
note 19.

[20] *Enchanted trifle* probably means *bewitching phantom.* *Enchanted* for
enchanting, in accordance with the usage, before noted, of active and passive
forms indiscriminately. See page 60, note 59. Walker, however, thinks
the meaning to be "some trifle *produced by enchantment* to abuse me." —
Abuse, both verb and substantive, was often used in the sense of *deceive,*
delude, or *cheat.*

Beats, as of flesh and blood ; and, since I saw thee,
Th' affliction of my mind amends, with which,
I fear, a madness held me : this must crave —
An if this be at all [21] — a most strange story.
Thy dukedom I resign [22] and do entreat
Thou pardon me my wrongs. [23]   But how should Prospero
Be living and be here ?
    Pros.   First, noble friend,
Let me embrace thine age, whose honour cannot
Be measured or confined.
    Gonza.   Whether this be
Or be not, I'll not swear.
    Pros.   You do yet taste
Some subtilties [24] o' the isle, that will not let you
Believe things certain. — Welcome, my friends all : —
[*Aside to* SEBAS. *and* ANTO.] But you, my brace of lords,
    were I so minded,
I here could pluck his Highness' frown upon you,
And justify you traitors : [25] at this time
I'll tell no tales.
    Sebas. [*Aside to* ANTO.] The Devil speaks in him.

---

    [21] That is, if there be any reality in all this. *An if*, again, as before explained. See page 96, note 20.
    [22] The dukedom of Milan had been made tributary to Naples by Antonio, as the price of aid in his usurpation.
    [23] Still another instance of the construction mentioned in note 3 of this scene. "*My* wrongs" may mean either the wrongs I have *done*, or the wrongs I have *suffered*.   Here it means the former.
    [24] *Subtilties* are quaint deceptive inventions; the word is common to ancient cookery, in which a disguised or ornamented dish is so termed. Fabyan's *Chronicle*, 1542, describes one made of pastry, " called a pelican sitting on his nest with his birds, and an image of Saint Catharine holding a book, and disputing with the doctors."
    [25] "*Prove* you traitors," or, " justify myself for calling you such."

Pros.   Now,
For you, most wicked sir, whom to call brother
Would even infect my mouth, I do forgive
Thy rankest fault; all of them; and require
My dukedom of thee, which perforce,[26] I know,
Thou must restore.

    Alon.   If thou be'st Prospero,
Give us particulars of thy preservation;
How thou hast met us here, who three hours since
Were wreck'd upon this shore; where I have lost —
How sharp the point of this remembrance is! —
My dear son Ferdinand.

    Pros.   I'm woe[27] for't, sir.

    Alon. Irreparable is the loss; and patience
Says it is past her cure.

    Pros.   I rather think
You have not sought her help; of whose soft grace,
For the like loss I have her sovereign aid,
And rest myself content.

    Alon.   You the like loss!

    Pros. As great to me, as late;[28] and, portable
To make the dear loss, have I means much weaker
Than you may call to comfort you; for I
Have lost my daughter.

    Alon. A daughter!
O Heavens, that they were living both in Naples,
The King and Queen there! that they were, I wish

    [26] *Perforce* is *of force*, that is, necessarily or of necessity.

    [27] *Woe* was often used thus with an adjective sense; *sorry.*

    [28] "As great to me, *and* as *recent.*" Or the meaning may be, "As great
to me as *it is* recent." Either explanation suits, but I prefer the first. —
Portable is *endurable.* The Poet has it repeatedly.

Myself were mudded in that oozy bed
Where my son lies.   When did you lose your daughter?

   Pros. . In this last tempest.   I perceive, these lords
At this encounter do so much admire,[29]
That they devour their reason, and scarce think
Their eyes do offices of truth, these words
Are natural breath : [30] but, howsoe'er you have
Been justled from your senses, know for certain
That I am Prospero, and that very Duke
Which was thrust forth of Milan ; who most strangely
Upon this shore, where you were wreck'd, was landed,
To be the lord on't.   No more yet of this ; [31]
For 'tis a chronicle of day by day,
Not a relation for a breakfast, nor
Befitting this first meeting.   Welcome, sir ;
This cell's my Court : here have I few attendants,
And subjects none abroad : pray you, look in.
My dukedom since you've given me again,
I will requite you with as good a thing ;
At least bring forth a wonder to content ye
As much as me my dukedom.

The entrance of the Cell opens, and discovers FERDINAND *and*
            MIRANDA *playing at chess.*

   Mira. Sweet lord, you play me false.
   Ferd.   No, my dear'st love,
I would not for the world.

   [29] Shakespeare commonly uses *admire* and its derivatives in the Latin
sense; that of *wonder* or *amazement*. The meaning here is, that their reason
is swallowed up in wonder.
   [30] " That these words which I am speaking are the words of a real living
man."
   [31] No more of this *now*, or *for the present*. So *yet* was often used.

Mira. Yes, for a score of kingdoms you should wrangle,[32]
And I would call it fair play.

Alon.   If this prove
A vision of the island, one dear son
Shall I twice lose.[33]

Sebas.   A most high miracle !

Ferd. Though the seas threaten, they are merciful !
I've cursed them without cause.   [*Kneels to* ALON.

Alon.   Now all the blessings
Of a glad father compass thee about !
Arise, and say how thou camest here.

Mira.   O, wonder !
How many goodly creatures are there here !
How beauteous mankind is !   O brave new world,
That has such people in't !

Pros.   'Tis new to thee.

Alon. What is this maid with whom thou wast at play?
Your eld'st acquaintance cannot be three hours :
Is she the goddess that hath sever'd us,
And brought us thus together?

[32] The sense evidently wanted here is, "you *might play me false*"; but
how to get this out of *wrangle*, is not very apparent.   Was *wrangle* used as
a technical term in chess and other games ?   In *King Henry V.*, i. 2, we
have this: "He hath made a match with such a *wrangler*, that all the Courts
of France will be disturb'd with chases."   This is said with reference to the
game of tennis; and *wrangler* here seems to mean *opponent* or *antagonist*.
Wrangle, however, is from the same original as *wrong*, and its radical-sense
is the same.   Mr. Joseph Crosby thinks the word is used here in this its
radical sense.   He writes me as follows: "In the North of England, *wrang-
dom* is a common word for *wrong*, and *wrangously* for *wrongfully*.   *Wrangle*
in this sentence is an explanatory parallelism of Miranda's 'play me false,'
and means *wrong me*, — cheat me in the game."

[33] "Shall *twice* lose" appears to mean "shall lose a *second time*."   He
has in effect lost his son once in supposing him drowned; and will lose him
again in the dispelling of the vision, if vision it should prove.

Ferd.   Sir, she's mortal ;
But by immortal Providence she's mine :
I chose her when I could not ask my father
For his advice, nor thought I had one. She
Is daughter to this famous Duke of Milan,
Of whom so often I have heard renown,
But never saw before ; of whom I have
Received a second life ; and second father
This lady makes him to me.
    Alon.   I am hers :
But, O, how oddly will it sound that I
Must ask my child forgiveness !
    Pros.   There, sir, stop :
Let us not burden our remembrance with
A heaviness that's gone.
    Gonza.   I've inly wept,
Or should have spoke ere this. — Look down, you gods,
And on this couple drop a blessèd crown !
For it is you that have chalk'd forth the way
Which brought us hither.
    Alon.   I say, Amen, Gonzalo !
    Gonza. Was Milan thrust from Milan, that his issue
Should become Kings of Naples ! O, rejoice
Beyond a common joy ! and set it down
With gold on lasting pillars : In one voyage
Did Claribel her husband find at Tunis ;
And Ferdinand, her brother, found a wife
Where he himself was lost ; Prospero, his dukedom,
In a poor isle ; and all of us, ourselves,
When no man was his own.[34]

    [34] When no man was *in his senses*, or had self-possession.

Alon. [*To* FERD. *and* MIRA.]   Give me your hands :
Let grief and sorrow still embrace his heart
That doth not wish you joy !
  Gonza.   Be't so ! Amen !—

Re-enter ARIEL, *with the* Master *and* Boatswain *amazedly following.*

O, look, sir, look, sir ! here is more of us :
I prophesied, if a gallows were on land,
This fellow could not drown.— Now, blasphemy,
That swear'st grace o'erboard, not an oath on shore ?
Hast thou no mouth by land ?   What is the news ?
  Boats. The best news is, that we have safely found
Our King and company ; the next, our ship —
Which, but three glasses since, we gave out split —
Is tight, and yare, and bravely rigg'd, as when
We first put out to sea.
  Ari. [*Aside to* PROS.]   Sir, all this service
Have I done since I went.
  Pros. [*Aside to* ARIEL.]   My tricksy [35] spirit !
  Alon. These are not natural events ; they strengthen
From strange to stranger.— Say, how came you hither ?
  Boats. If I did think, sir, I were well awake,
I'd strive to tell you.   We were dead of sleep,
And — how we know not — all clapp'd under hatches ;
Where, but even now, with strange and several noises
Of roaring, shrieking, howling, jingling chains,
And more diversity of sounds, all horrible,
We were awaked ; straightway, at liberty :
When we, in all her trim, freshly beheld

[35] Ariel seems to be called *tricksy*, because his execution has the celerity
of magic, or of a juggler's tricks : " clever, adroit, dexterous," says Dyce.

Our royal, good, and gallant ship ; our master
Capering to eye her : [36] on a trice, so please you,
Even in a dream, were we divided from them,
And were brought moping [37] hither.

    Ari. [*Aside to* Pros.]   Was't well done?

    Pros. [*Aside to* Ari.] Bravely, my diligence. Thou shalt
      be free.

    Alon. This is as strange a maze as e'er men trod ;
And there is in this business more than Nature
Was ever conduct of : [38] some oracle
Must rectify our knowledge.

    Pros.   Sir, my liege,
Do not infest your mind with beating on [39]
The strangeness of this business ; at pick'd leisure,
Which shall be shortly, single I'll resolve [40] you —
Which to you shall seem probable — of every
These happen'd accidents : till when, be cheerful,
And think of each thing well. — [*Aside to* Ariel.] Come
      hither, spirit :
Set Caliban and his companions free ;
Untie the spell. [*Exit* Ari.] — How fares my gracious sir?
There are yet missing of your company
Some few odd lads that you remember not.

    [36] "Capering *to eye* her" is leaping or dancing with joy *at seeing* her.
Still another instance of the infinitive used gerundively.

    [37] To *mope* is to be *dull* or *stupid;* originally, *dim-sighted.*

    [38] *Conduct* for *conductor;* that is, *guide* or *leader.* Often so.

    [39] We have a like expression in use now, — "Still hammering at it."

    [40] In Shakespeare, to *resolve* often means to *satisfy,* or to *explain satis-
factorily.* — *Single* appears to be used adverbially here, its force going with
the predicate ; and the last *which* refers to *resolve :* "I will explain to you
—and the explanation shall seem to you natural and likely—all these incidents, *severally,* or *in detail,* as they have happened."

Re-enter ARIEL, *driving in* CALIBAN, STEPHANO, *and* TRIN-
CULO, *in their stolen apparel.*

Steph. Every man shift for all the rest,[41] and let no man
take care for himself; for all is but fortune. — Coragio, bully-
monster, coragio !

Trin. If these be true spies which I wear in my head,
here's a goodly sight.

Cal. O Setebos, these be brave spirits indeed !
How fine my master is !   I am afraid
He will chastise me.

Sebas. Ha, ha !
What things are these, my Lord Antonio?
Will money buy 'em?

Anto.   Very like ; one of them
Is a plain fish, and, no doubt, marketable.

Pros. Mark but the badges of these men, my lords,
Then say if they be true.   This mis-shaped knave, —
His mother was a witch ; and one so strong
That could control the Moon, make flows and ebbs,
And deal in her command without her power.[42]
These three have robb'd me ; and this demi-devil —
For he's a bastard one — had plotted with them
To take my life : two of these fellows you
Must know and own ; this thing of darkness I
Acknowledge mine.

---

[41] Stephano's tongue is rather tipsy still, and staggers into a misplacement of his words. He means " Let every man shift for himself."

[42] *Without* has here the sense of *beyond;* a common usage in the Poet's
time. So in *A Midsummer-Night's Dream,* iv. 1 : " Where we might be *without* the peril of th' Athenian law." And in Jonson's *Cynthia's Revels,* i. 4:
" O, now I apprehend you : your phrase was *without* me before." So that
the meaning of the text is, " who could outdo the Moon in exercising the
Moon's own command."

Cal.   I shall be pinch'd to death.

Alon. Is not this Stephano, my drunken butler?

Sebas. He is drunk now : where had he wine?

Alon. And Trinculo is reeling ripe : where should they
Find this grand liquor that hath gilded [43] 'em?—
How camest thou in this pickle?

Trin. I have been in such a pickle since I saw you last,
that, I fear me, will never out of my bones : I shall not fear
fly-blowing. [44]

Sebas. Why, how now, Stephano !

Steph. O, touch me not ! I am not Stephano. but a
cramp.

Pros. You'd be king o' the isle, sirrah?

Steph. I should have been a sore [45] one, then.

Alon. [*Pointing to* CAL.] This is as strange a thing a•
e'er I look'd on.

Pros. He is as disproportion'd in his manners
As in his shape. — Go, sirrah, to my cell ;

---

[43] The phrase *being gilded* was a trite one for being drunk; perhaps
from the effect of liquor in colouring the face, but more likely because
drinking puts one into *golden altitudes.* It has been suggested, also, that
there is an allusion to the *grand elixir* of the alchemists, which was an ideal
medicine for *gilding* a base metal in the sense of *transmuting it into gold;*
as also for repairing health and prolonging life in man. This, too, is probable enough; for the Poet is fond of clustering various ideas round a single
image.

[44] Trinculo is playing rather deeply upon *pickle;* and one of the senses
here intended is that of being pickled in salt or brine so as not to become
tainted. *Fly-blows* are the maggot-eggs deposited by flies; and to *fly-blow*
is to taint with such eggs.

[45] A pun upon the different senses of *sore*, one of which is *harsh, severe,*
or *oppressive.* The same equivoque occurs in *2 Henry the Sixth,* iv. 7, where
Dick proposes that Cade's mouth be the source of English law, and John
remarks, aside, — " Mass, 'twill be a *sore* law, then; for he was thrust in the
mouth with a spear, and 'tis not whole yet."

Take with you your companions ; as you look
To have my pardon, trim it handsomely.

   Cal. Ay, that I will ; and I'll be wise hereafter,
And seek for grace.   What a thrice double ass
Was I, to take this drunkard for a god,
And worship this dull fool !

   Pros.   Go to ; away !

   Alon. Hence, and bestow your luggage where you found it.

   Sebas. Or stole it, rather.

              [*Exeunt* CAL., STEPH., *and* TRIN.

   Pros. Sir, I invite your Highness and your train
To my poor cell, where you shall take your rest
For this one night ; which, part of it, I'll waste
With such discourse as, I not doubt, shall make it
Go quick away, — the story of my life,
And the particular accidents gone by,
Since I came to this isle : and in the morn
I'll bring you to your ship, and so to Naples,
Where I have hope to see. the nuptial
Of these our dear-belovèd solemnized ;
And thence retire me [46] to my Milan, where
Every third thought shall be my grave.

   Alon.   I long
To hear the story of your life, which must
Take the ear strangely.

   Pros.   I'll deliver all ;
And promise you calm seas, auspicious gales,
And sail so expeditious, that shall catch
Your royal fleet far off. — [*Aside to* ARI.]   My Ariel,
    chick,

   [46] That is, *withdraw myself.* The Poet has various instances of *retire*
thus used as a transitive verb.

That is thy charge : then to the elements
Be free, and fare thou well ! — Please you, draw near.

                               [Exeunt

EPILOGUE.

SPOKEN BY PROSPERO.

Now my charms are all o'erthrown,
And what strength I have's mine own, —
Which is most faint : now, 'tis true,
I must be here confined by you,
Or sent to Naples. Let me not,
Since I have my dukedom got,
And pardon'd the deceiver, dwell
In this bare island by your spell ;
But release me from my bands,
With the help of your good hands.[47]
Gentle breath of yours my sails
Must fill, or else my project fails,
Which was to please : now I want
Spirits to enforce, art to enchant ;
And my ending is despair,
Unless I be relieved by prayer ;
Which pierces so, that it assaults
Mercy itself, and frees all faults.
As you from crimes would pardon'd be,
Let your indulgence set me free.

[47] The Epilogue is supposed to be addressed to the theatrical audience,
and the speaker here solicits their applause by the clapping of their hands.
Noise was a breaker of enchantments and spells; hence the applause would
release him from his bonds.

CRITICAL NOTES.

ACT I., SCENE I.

Page 44. *Blow, till thou burst* thy *wind*, &c. — Steevens conjectured "Blow, till thou burst *thee*, wind." This accords with a similar passage in *King Lear*, iii. 2: "Blow, winds, and crack your cheeks!" See, however, foot-note 3.

P. 45. *Bring her to try wi' th' main-course.* — In the original, "bring her to Try with Maine-course"; which leaves us in doubt as to how the clause should be punctuated. Mr. Grant White, at the suggestion of Mr. W. W. Story, prints "Bring her to: try wi' th' main-course"; and quotes the following from Lord Mulgrave, a sailor critic: "The gale increasing, the topmast is struck, to take the weight from aloft, make the ship drive less to leeward, and bear the mainsail, under which the ship is *brought to*." The likelihoods seem about evenly balanced between the two ways of printing the passage. Of the more recent editors, Collier, Staunton, Singer, and Dyce punctuate as in the text. See foot-note 9.

P. 47. Ling, *heath*, broom, *furze, any thing.* — The original has "*Long* heath, *Browne* firrs." But it does not appear that there are or ever were any plants known as *long heath* and *brown furze*. The reading in the text is Hanmer's, and has the unqualified approval of Walker; who observes, "The balance requires it. Besides, what are *long heath* and *brown furze?*" See foot-note 17.

149

ACT I., SCENE I.

P. 48.   *A brave vessel,*
Who had no doubt some noble creatures *in her.* — So Theobald
and Collier's second folio: the original has *creature* instead of *creatures.*

P. 50. *I have with such* prevision *in mine art.* — The old text has
provision. The change is from Collier's second folio, and accords
with what Ariel says in ii. 1: "My master through his art *foresees* the
danger that you, his friend, are in."

P. 51.   *And thy father*
Was Duke of Milan; thou his only heir,
A princess, — no worse issued. — The old text reads "*and* his
onely heire"; the *and* being evidently repeated by mistake from the
preceding line. Steevens made the correction. The original also has
"*And* Princesse; no worse Issued." Corrected by Pope. The old
copies have various instances of *and* thus misprinted for *a.* So in
King Henry VIII., ii. 4: "On the debating *And* Marriage 'twixt the
Duke of Orleance and Our daughter Mary."

P. 53. *The ivy which had hid my princely trunk,*
And suck'd the verdure out on't. — The original reads "Suck'd
my verdure"; the *my* being probably repeated by mistake from the
preceding line.

P. 53.   *Like one*
Who having unto truth, by falsing of it,
Made such a sinner of his memory,
To credit his own lie. — The old copies read "having *into*
truth, by *telling* of it." This reading, with *unto* substituted for *into*, is
commonly explained by making *it* refer to *lie* in the second line after.
But is this, or was it ever, a legitimate English construction? Collier's
second folio substitutes *to untruth* for *into truth;* rather plausibly, at
first sight. But the meaning in that case would be, "having made his

memory a *sinner* to *untruth* by lying"; whereas the sense required clearly is, "having made his memory a sinner unto *truth* by lying." This sense is aptly expressed by *falsing*, as, I think, every one will see. Nor does it seem to me at all unlikely that *tell* should have been misprinted for *fals;* especially as the verb to *false* was passing out of use before 1623. The quotations given in foot-note 27 appear to yield the present reading ample support; but, as several eminent Shake-spearians with whom I have corresponded object to it, I here add a few others. So in *The Faerie Queene,* i. 9, 46: —

> Is not enough, that to this Lady mild
> Thou *falsèd* hast thy faith with perjuree?

Also, in the same, ii. 5, 9: —

> Sometimes athwart, sometimes he strook him strayt,
> And *falsèd* oft his blowes t' illude him with such bayt.

Also, in the Epilogue to *The Shepheards Calendar :* —

> To teach the ruder shepheard how to feede his sheepe,
> And from the *falsers* fraud his folded flocke to keepe.

Also, in Daniel's *Complaint of Rosamond :* —

> Such one was I, my beauty was mine own;
>   No borrow'd blush, which bankrupt beauties seek,
> That new-found shame, a sin to us unknown, —
> Th' adulterate beauty of a *falsèd* cheek.

As to the other change, *unto* for *into,* it appears that these two forms were often used indiscriminately; at all events, the old editions often have *into* where our present idiom absolutely requires *unto.* So in *Cymbeline,* i. 6: "Such a holy witch, that he enchants societies *into* him." And, as an instance of the converse, in *A Midsummer-Night's Dream,* i. 1, the quartos read, "That he hath turn'd a heaven *unto* a hell"; while the folio has "a heaven *into* a hell."

But the Rev. Mr. Arrowsmith has lately proposed an ingenious application of the old text, which seems to call for some notice. He thinks the right construction to be, "by telling of it into truth." And he quotes several instances of like expression; as the following from South's Sermons: "Till he has *thought a distasteful apprehension into an action of murder.*" And again: "Yet *vice cannot be praised into virtue.*" This form of speech is not indeed uncommon, and it has long been familiar to me ; but I cannot think the cases parallel. In that construction of the passage the pronoun *it* must refer to some antecedent, and cannot be used absolutely, as it well may be in the reading here given ; yet there is nothing for it to refer to, at least nothing but *lie*, in the second line after, which is, I think, inadmissible, for the reason already stated. Moreover, the sense of *telling a lie into truth* seems to me quite unsuited to the place. In short, this explanation is so strained and far-fetched, that it only operates with me as a further argument against the old text.

P. 54. *To have no screen between this part he play'd*
    And them *he play'd it for, he needs will be*
    Absolute Milan. — The original reads "And *him* he play'd it for." The correction is Mr. P. A. Daniel's, and seems to me eminently judicious. I never could make any sense out of the old text. See foot-note 31.

P. 55. Mira.   *I should sin*
    To think but nobly of my grandmother.
          Pros. *Good wombs have borne bad sons.* — In the old text, the last line is made a part of Miranda's speech. Theobald thought it should be as here given, and so Hanmer printed it.

P. 55.   *One midnight*
    Fated to th' practice *did Antonio open*
    The gates of Milan ; and, i' the dead of darkness,
    The ministers for th' purpose hurried thence
    Me and thy crying self. — The original has "Fated to th' *purpose.*" The change is from Collier's second folio, and is admitted on the ground that *purpose* may have got repeated by mistake from the second line after. Staunton thinks it "an improvement," and Dyce adopts it. Still I do not feel quite sure about it.

P. 55. *I, not remembering how I cried* on't *then,*
    Will cry it o'er again. — The original has "how I cried *out* then"; which gives nothing for *it*, in the next line, to refer to. Lettsom would read "how I cried *it* then."

P. 56.   *Dear, they durst not —*
So dear the love my people bore me — set
A mark so bloody on the business. — The original has "*nor* set
A marke." The *nor* both spoils the metre, and, to say the least, hurts
the sense. The omission was proposed by Mr. William Aldis Wright.

P. 56.   *Where they prepared*
A rotten carcass of a boat, not rigg'd,
Nor tackle, sail, nor mast ; the very rats
Instinctively had *quit it.* — The original has *butt* instead of
boat, and, in the last line, *have* instead of *had.*

P. 56.   *Thou didst smile,*
Infus'd with a fortitude from Heaven,
When I have degg'd *the sea with drops full salt.* — The original
reads " When I have *deck'd* the sea." The word *deck'd* has given the
editors a deal of trouble ; and no wonder, for neither of its admitted
senses at all suits the context. Dyce, I think, was the first to suggest
that it might be " a corruption of the provincialism *degg'd,* that is, *sprin-
kled.*" See foot-note 44.

P. 57. *Some food we had, and some fresh water, that*
A noble Neapolitan, Gonzalo,
Out of his charity, — being then appointed
Master of this design, — did give us. — The original has "*who*
being then appointed." The pronoun *who* upsets both grammar and
metre, and also obscures the sense. Pope omits it.

P. 59.   *Jove's* lightnings, *the precursors*
O' the dreadful thunder claps, more momentary
And sight-outrunning were not : the fire, and cracks
Of sulphurous roaring, the most mighty Neptune
Seem'd *to besiege,* &c. — The original has *lightning* for *light-
nings,* and " *Seeme* to besiege."

P. 60. *On their* unstaining *garments not a blemish,*
But fresher than before. — The old text has " on their *sustain-
ing* garments "; which cannot well be explained to any fitting sense.

Probably the Poet's language was sophisticated by the transcriber or
the printer, not understanding the old indiscriminate use of active and
passive forms. Since the change was made, I learn that Mr. Sped-
ding had conjectured the same reading. See foot-note 59.'

P. 62. Pros. *What is the time o' the day?*
      Ariel.   *Past the mid season,*
  At least two glasses.
      Pros.   *The time 'twixt six and now*
Must by us both be spent most preciously. — The old copies print
"At least two glasses" as a part of Prospero's next speech. Cor-
rected by Warburton.

P. 62. *Told thee no lies, made no mistakings.* — The original has
"made *thee* no mistakings"; where *thee* spoils the verse without helping
the sense. Doubtless an accidental repetition from the preceding clause.

P. 63.   *For one thing she* had,
    They would not take her life. — The original reads "For one
thing she *did.*" This is, to say the least, very obscure, and there is
nothing in the play that throws any light upon it. The reading in the
text is explained by what Prospero says in his next speech: "This
blue-eyed hag was hither brought *with child,*" &c. The correction was
proposed to me by Mr. Joseph Crosby.

P. 64. *Go make thyself like to a nymph o' the sea :*
    Be subject to no sight but mine. — The original reads, "most
ridiculously," says Dyce, "no sight but *thine and* mine." It also omits
to after *like.* Supplied in the second folio.

P. 65.   *Go take this shape;*
    And hither come in't: hence with diligence! — So Hanmer.
The original repeats *go* before *hence;* thus spoiling the metre to no
purpose.

P. 65. *Come forth, I say! there's other business for thee :*
    Come forth, *thou tortoise!* — The original omits the second
forth. Both sense and metre evidently require it to be repeated along
with *Come.* Inserted by Steevens.

P. 65. *As* wicked *dew as e'er my mother brush'd*

  With raven's feather from unwholesome fen. — Upon this Dyce notes as follows: "Though *wicked*, as an epithet of *dew*, makes very good sense, (meaning baleful,) I suspect that it is not Shakespeare's word, and that it has been repeated by mistake from the line just above." Perhaps the Poet wrote *cursed*.

P. 66.   *A south-west blow on ye,*

  And blister you all o'er. — Ought it not to be "A south-west *wind* blow on ye"? It seems to me that both sense and metre call for *wind*. And where two or more consecutive words begin with the same or similar letters, one is very apt to drop out.

P. 66.   *When thou camest* here *first,*

  Thou strokedst me and madest much of me. — The old text is without *here*. Ritson thought the word ought to be supplied; and Walker says, "'camest *here* first,' surely."

P. 68.   *Therefore wast thou*

  Deservedly *confined into this rock,*

  Who hadst deserved more than a prison. — I suspect, with Walker, that *deservedly* crept into the text from some other hand than Shakespeare's. Walker observes that "the nine-syllable line is alien to Shakespeare," and proposes to print as follows, adding, "Note the difference of the flow": —

> Therefore wast thou
> Confined into this rock, who hadst deserved
> More than a prison.

P. 69. *Curtsied when you have, and kiss'd*

  The wild waves whist,

  Foot it featly here and there. — So printed in the original. Dyce, with most of the modern editors, makes the second line parenthetical, thus: —

> Curtsied when you have and kiss'd, —
> The wild waves whist, — &c.

This of course means "the wild waves *being* whist." *Whist,* I suppose, means *still* or *calm ;* and how the waves could be *wild* and *calm* at the same time, does not well appear. Besides, Dyce's mode of printing, it seems to me, expunges a delicate touch of poetry that is well worth keeping. See foot-note 89.

P. 69. *Hark, hark! the watch-dogs bark*, &c. — I here adopt the reading and arrangement proposed by Mr. P. A. Daniel; which, I think, fairly extricate the latter part of Ariel's song from all difficulty. In the original it stands thus: —

> *Foote it featly heere, and there, and sweete Sprights beare*
> *the burthen.*   Burthen dispersedly.
> *Harke, harke, bowgh wawgh :   the watch-Dogges barke,*
> *bowgh-wawgh.*
> Ar. *Hark, hark, I heare, the straine of strutting Chanticlere*
> *cry cockadidle-dowe.*

Mr. Daniel comments upon the matter as follows: " Every reader will, I think, accept Pope's alteration of *beare the burthen* to *the burthen beare;* but there seems to be a diversity of opinion as to what that burthen is. Some editors only give *bowgh-wawgh, bowgh-wawgh,* as the burthen; others the whole line, *Harke, harke, bowgh-wawgh : the watch-dogges barke, bowgh-wawgh;* and all give *cry cockadidle-dowe* as part of Ariel's song. *Cry* seems to me to be merely a stage-direction. The burthen heard dispersedly is the barking of dogs and the crowing of cocks."

P. 73.   *What, I say,*
    My fool *my tutor?* — The original ha* *fo^* instead of *fool.* Walker says, " Read *fool,*" and quotes from Beaumont and Fletcher's *Pilgrim,* iv. 1: —

> When *fools* and mad-folks shall be *tutors to me,*
> And feel my sores, yet I unsensible, &c.

P. 74. *My father's loss, the weakness which I feel,*
    The wreck of all my friends, and *this man's threats*
    To whom I am subdued, are light to me. — The original reads " *nor* this man's threats," and " are *but* light to me "; of which the one plainly upsets the sense, and the other the metre.

ACT II., SCENE I.

P. 76. *I pr'ythee spare* me. — So Walker. The original lacks *me*.

P. 77. Adri. *Though this island seem to be desert,* —
Sebas. *Ha, ha, ha ! — So, you're paid.*
Adri. — *uninhabitable,* &c. — The original prints the second line as two speeches, and assigns the latter part, "So, you're paid," to Antonio. Mr. White changes *you're paid* to *you've paid.* The correction in the text is Theobald's. See foot-note 5.

P. 79. Alon. *Ah !* — The original has " *Gon.*" instead of " *Alon.*" The correction is Staunton's ; who notes, " this exclamation belongs to Alonso, who is awakened from his trance of grief."

P. 81. *And the fair soul herself*
Weigh'd, between loathness and obedience, at
Which end the *beam should bow.* — The original reads " at Which end *o' the* beam should bow." Modern editions generally change *should* to *she'd ;* but it seems to me much better to erase *o',* and thus make *beam* the subject of *should bow.* Pope's correction.

P. 83. Sebas. God *save his Majesty !*
Anto. *Long live Gonzalo !* — So Walker. The original omits *God,* which was probably stricken out by the Master of the Revels in obedience to the well-known statute against profanity. In such matters, the Poet's judgment seems preferable to an Act of Parliament. The folio has many instances of such omission, where the quartos which were printed before the passing of the Act in question give the text as Shakespeare undoubtedly wrote it.

P. 84. *Will you laugh me asleep ? for I am very heavy.*
Anto. *Go sleep, and hear us* not. — The original is without *not.* There appears no assignable reason of wit why the Poet should have left it out, and all other reasons certainly require it. Keightly's correction.

P. 87. *Ambition cannot pierce a wink beyond,*—

But doubt *discovery there.* — Here Capell substitutes *doubts* for *doubt*, but, as it seems to me, without at all relieving the obscurity. Hanmer reads "But *drops* discovery there." This is more intelligible, but still unsatisfactory. The passage has long been a poser to me, as I have met with no sufficient explanation of it. Possibly we ought to read "*Nor aught discover* there." See foot-note 42.   .

P. 87. *She that is Queen of Tunis; she that dwells*
   Ten leagues beyond man's life; she that from Naples
   Can have no note, unless the Sun were post,—
   The Man-i'-the-moon's too slow,— *till new-born chins*
   Be rough and razorable. She 'twas for *whom* we
   All were sea-swallow'd, though some cast again;

And, by that destiny, to perform an act, &c.— In the old text, the fifth of these lines stands precisely thus: " Be rough, and Razor-able: She that from whom." The modern text is, " Be rough and razorable; she that from whom," or " she from whom," or " she from whom *coming.*" But these readings all seem to me to miss the essential point; for they proceed upon the supposal that what comes after *razorable* is in the same construction with what precedes; which appears quite at odds with the proper logic of the passage, and also with the right Shakespearian rhythm of thought and expression. And the old text rather looks as if a full stop were intended at *razorable*, and a new construction there to begin. On the other hand, however, in the old " She that from whom," *that* must needs be taken as a relative pronoun, just as it is in the preceding clauses. Now " she that from whom" is not English, and, I am sure, never was; for it is the same as " she *who* from whom," which is absurd. At one time I thought of reading " *She's* that from whom," which makes *that* a demonstrative pronoun, and thus removes the absurdity aforesaid. But it seems to me better to substitute *'twas,* and so get rid of *that* altogether. Nor is the change at all violent. And my theory is, that " she that from" got repeated by a sort of contagion from the third line above. As to the change of *from* into *for*, perhaps it is not strictly necessary, as *from* may possibly yield the same meaning. At all events, *for whom* legitimately carries the sense of *on whose account*, or, *because of whom. For* is often used thus. — In the old text, again, the pronoun *we* stands at the beginning of the sixth line, instead of at the end of the fifth. This change is made because, in the old arrangement, the proper rhythm of the sixth is spoiled, it being against all Shakespearian rules to set an extra syllable at the beginning of a verse ; whereas nothing is more common than such syllables at the end. See foot-note 45.

P. 88.   *A space whose every cubit*
   Seems to cry out, "How shalt thou, Claribel,
   Measure us back to Naples? Keep in Tunis,
   And let Sebastian wake!" — The original reads "How *shall that* Claribel Measure," &c. The reading here given is Hanmer's. I am surprised that it has not been more generally accepted; for the continuation of the speech, "Keep in Tunis," &c., is clearly an apostrophe to Claribel, and was no doubt meant to be in the same construction.

P. 89. Sebas. *But, for your conscience —*
   Anto. *Ay, sir; and where lies that? if 'twere a kibe,*
   'Twould put me to my slipper. — The original is without *and* in the second of these lines. Inserted by Dyce.

P. 89.   *Here lies your brother,*
   No better than the earth he lies upon,
   If he were that which now he's like; whom I,
   With this obedient steel, three inches of it,
   Can lay to bed for ever. — In the third of these lines, the original has *that's dead* after "now he's like," and transfers *whom I* to the beginning of the next line. Steevens made the following just note upon the passage: "The words *that's dead* (as Dr. Farmer observes to me) are evidently a gloss, or marginal note, which has found its way into the text. Such a supplement is useless to the speaker's meaning, and the next verse becomes redundant by its insertion."

P. 90. *My master through his art foresees the danger*
   That you, his friend, are in; and sends me forth —
   For else his project dies — to keep thee *living.* — The original reads "to keepe *them* living." Some editors change *project* to *projects*, and thus make an antecedent for *them;* but Dyce's correction is unquestionably right.

P. 90. Gon. [Waking.]   *Now, good angels*

    Preserve the King!—[To SEBAS. and ANTO.] *Why, how now!—*
    [To ALON.]   *Ho, awake!*
    [To SEBAS. and ANTO.]   *Why are you drawn? wherefore this*
      ghastly looking?

    Alon. [Waking.]   *What's the matter?*—I here give the arrangement which Dyce adopted and improved from Staunton. The old text makes a strange muddle of the passage, thus:—

> *Gon.* Now, good Angels preserve the King.
> *Alon.* Why how now hoa; awake? why are you drawn?
> Wherefore this ghastly looking?
> *Gon.* What's the matter?

P. 91. *I saw their weapons drawn: there was a noise,*

    That's verity.—Instead of *verity*, the original has *verily*. Corrected by Pope.

ACT II., SCENE II.

P. 96. *Here; swear, man, how thou escapedst.*—The old text reads "swere *then* how thou escap'dst." This makes the speech addressed to Caliban, whereas the context clearly requires it to be addressed to Trinculo. Several ways of printing have been proposed, in order to get over the difficulty; but they only remove one difficulty to draw on another. Probably the transcriber or compositor supposed the speech addressed to Caliban, and sophisticated it into logical harmony with that idea, by changing *man* into *then*.

P. 98.   *And sometimes I'll get thee*

    Young staniels *from the rock.*—Instead of *staniels*, the original has *scamels*, which has drawn forth a deal of commentary. The correction is Dyce's, from whose remarks on the passage I condense the following: "Here *scamels* has been explained as the diminutive of *scams*, and as meaning limpets. But I have little or no doubt that it is a misprint: for who gathers *young* limpets? and besides, the words *from the rock* would seem to be equivalent to *from the cliffs.* Theobald substituted *shamois*, and also proposed *sea-malls* or *sea-mells*, and *stannels* or *staniels.* In the first place, *staniels* comes very near the trace of the old letters. Secondly, *staniels* accords well with the context, 'from the rock'; for, as Montagu's *Ornithological Dictionary* tells us, the 'Kestrel, *Stannel*, or Windhover, is one of our most common species of hawks, especially in the more *rocky situations and high cliffs on our coasts, where they breed*.' Thirdly, in another passage of Shakespeare, where nobody doubts that the genuine reading is *staniel*, all the old editions exhibit the gross misprint, *stallion :* 'And with what wing the *stallion* checks at it!' *Twelfth Night,* ii. 5."

P. 98. *Nor scrape* trencher, *nor wash dish.* — The original has *trenchering,* "which," says Dyce, "is undoubtedly an error of the transcriber or compositor, occasioned by the preceding words *firing* and *requiring*." Pope's correction.

ACT III., SCENE I.

P. 99.   *This my mean task would be*
  As heavy to me as 'tis *odious, but*
    The mistress, &c. — The original lacks *'tis,* which was inserted by Pope ; and rightly, beyond question.

P. 99. *But these sweet thoughts do even refresh my* labour ;
    Most busy when I do it least. — The original has *labours* instead of *labour,* and also reads "Most busie *lest,* when I doe it." The second folio changes *lest* to *least*. But the two forms were often used indifferently, and either form was used in both the senses of our present words *lest* and *least*. Modern editions generally print *labour* instead of *labours,* so as to harmonize with *it* in the next line. Few passages in Shakespeare have been more fruitful of comment and controversy than this. The list of changes made or proposed is quite too long for reproduction here. With the old reading it is uncertain what *most busy* refers to or is the predicate of ; that is to say, whether the meaning be "*I being* most busy," or "these sweet *thoughts* being most busy." For the latter sense the best reading I have met with is "most *busiest,*" proposed by Holt White, and adopted by Singer and Grant White. But had this been the Poet's thought he would probably have written "Most busy *they,* when I do it." Dyce prints, with Theobald, "Most *busiless,*" which, of course, makes the phrase refer to the speaker

himself; but the reading is to me quite unsatisfactory. On the whole, it seems much better to connect *lest* or *least* with what follows, and not with what precedes. It is worth noting, also, that the old reading throws the ictus on *I* and *it*, whereas it ought, apparently, to fall on *when* and *do*. Hardly any corruptions are more frequent in Shakespeare than those resulting from misplacement of words, and even of whole lines. Many are the cases where similar transpositions have to be made. In this case we might read "Most busy, *least* when I do it"; but this gives us a very awkward inversion, and both sense and rhythm come much better by transposing *least* to the end. But I suspect, after all, that the Poet first wrote *most busie*, then interlined *lest* or *least* as a correction, and that the two got printed together; so that we ought to read "*Least* busy when I do it." And so Pope reads. — Perhaps I ought to add that Mr. A. E. Brae proposes to read "my *labour's* most busy *hest*"; *hest* being taken in the sense of *task* or *exaction*. With this reading, as the proposer observes, "an object is given to the possessive *s* in *labour's*, and an antecedent provided for the pronoun *it* in the last line." But this reading, I think, would make the passage rather too tame. See foot-note 2.

P. 103. *So glad of this as they I cannot be,*
    Who am surprised withal. — The old text reads "*Who are* surprised *with all.*" Theobald changed *with all* to *withal*, and rightly, beyond question. The same misprint occurs frequently, as Walker has shown. And so *are* is, I have no doubt, a misprint for *am*. Prospero is himself surprised, as indeed he well may be, that his wish has been crowned so far beyond his expectations; and it is most natural that he should be expressing that surprise: but the lovers, I take it, are not at all surprised at what has sprung up in their hearts; it seems to them the most natural thing in the world.

ACT III., SCENE II.

P. 105.   *Wilt thou be pleased*
    To hearken once again the suit I made thee? — The original prints this speech as prose, and reads "to hearken once again *to the* suit I made *to* thee." Caliban everywhere else, I believe, except in

his next speech, uses verse: it seems indeed one of his leading characteristics to do so. Dyce thinks the present speech should be printed
as in the text.

P. 107. *He has brave utensils, — for so he calls them, —*
 Which, when he has a house, he'll deck't *withal.* — So Hanmer
and Walker. The original, *decke* for *deck't.*

P. 108. *I ne'er saw woman,*
 But only Sycorax my dam and she. — The original reads " I
never saw *a* woman." Corrected by Pope.

P. 109. Cal. *The sound is going away; let's follow it,*
 And after do our work. — The old copies assign this speech to
Trinculo. The correction is Mr. P. A. Daniel's, who justly observes
that " Stephano replies to it, ' Lead, monster; we'll follow.' "

P. 110. Steph. *I would I could see this taborer! he lays it on.* —
Wilt come?
 Trin. *I'll follow, Stephano.* — Such is clearly the right distribution,
as Ritson observes. The old copies make *Wilt come* the beginning
of Trinculo's speech.

ACT III., SCENE III.

P. 113. *Each putter-out* of one *for* five. — The original inverts the
order here, *of five for one;* which can hardly be made to yield the
right sense. The correction is Thirlby's. See foot-note 12.

P. 114. *The never-surfeited sea*
 Hath caused to belch up; yea, and on this island,
 Where man doth not inhabit. — The original reads " to belch
up *you.*" But the object of *belch up* is expressed in *whom,* fourth line
above; the regular construction being, " You are three men of sin,
whom Destiny hath caused the never-surfeited sea to belch up." So
that *you* coming in after *belch up* is, to say the least, extremely awkward. And, as we have *you* again in the next line, right under *yea,*
the misprint, if it be one, is easily accounted for. The correction is
Staunton's.

P. 116.   *Their great guilt,*
    Like poison given to work a long *time after.* — The original
reads "work a *great* time after." — The change is Walker's, who sup-
poses *great* to have been repeated by mistake from the preceding line.

ACT IV., SCENE I.

P. 117.   *As I hope*
    For quiet days, fair issue, and long life,
    With love such as 'tis now, the murkiest even,
    The most oppórtune place, the strong'st suggestion
Our worser genius can, &c. — The old text has "the murkiest
den." The reading *even* or *e'en* for *den* was proposed by "C. T." in
Notes and Queries, July 25, 1874. The natural logic of the passage
plainly requires some word denoting time; as the speaker is apparently supposing a concurrence of the several inducements of time,
place, and inclination. Besides, the sense of "murkiest den" is better
expressed in "most oppórtune place." The misprint of *d* for *e* occurs,
I think, oftener than any other.

P. 119. *Thy banks with* peonéd *and* twilléd *brims,*
        Which spongy April at thy hest betrims,
    To make cold nymphs chaste crowns. — The first of these lines has
proved, with one exception, more fruitful of comment and controversy
than any other passage in the play. Those who retain the old reading
commonly explain *peoned* or *pioned* as meaning *dug,* and *twilled* as meaning *ridged,* or made into ridges, — a sense which it bears in reference
to some kinds of cloth. But the words so explained will nowise cohere
with the purpose assigned, "to make cold nymphs chaste crowns."
Others understand *peoned* as referring to the well-known flower called
peony, and change *twilled* to *lilied.* This gives a meaning in harmony
with the context indeed, but hardly consistent with fact: for, though
it appears from Bacon's essay *Of Gardens* that peonies and lilies
bloomed in April, it nowhere appears that those flowers bloomed, or
even grew, in such places as the brims of rivers. In fact, the peony,
as it is known to us, is not a wild flower, does not grow in marshy
grounds, and has no connection with river-banks. The difficulty, I

think, is fairly cleared up by *The Edinburgh Review* for October, 1872. The learned writer has the following: "We could not but believe that there must be some flower, most probably a water-flower, or one living on marshy ground, that was provincially known as a peony. In confirmation of this view, we were informed by a clergyman who was for many years incumbent of a parish in the county, that *peony* is the name given in Warwickshire to the marsh-marigold. On a little reflection it was not difficult to see why the name of the peony should have been transferred to the marsh-marigold. In their early stages, when the peculiar state of the bud naturally attracts attention, the peony and marsh-marigold are alike, not only in growth and form, but in colour also. The marsh-marigold haunts the watery margins as the constant associate of reeds and rushes, blooms in 'spongy April,' and, in common with other water flowers, is twined with sedge 'to make cold nymphs chaste crowns.'". The writer also quotes from Mrs. Loudon's description of the flower: "This is one of the most showy of the British plants, and it is also one of the most common, as there are few ponds or slow rivers in Great Britain that have not some of these plants growing on their banks in April and May." In regard to *twillèd* also, the same writer shows that *twills* was an old provincial name for *reeds* and certain species of *sedge*. "The word is indeed," says he, "still retained in its secondary application, being commercially used to denote the fluted or rib-like effect produced on various fabrics by a kind of ridged or carded weaving. *Twillèd* is, therefore, the very word to describe the crowded sedges in the shallower reaches of the Avon as it winds around Stratford." On the whole, then, I am satisfied that the old reading must stand; though, without the foregoing explanation, I was never able to see any sense in it. See foot-note 14.

P. 120.   *And thy* brown *groves,*

    Whose shadow the dismissèd bachelor loves. — So Hanmer and Collier's second folio. The original has " thy *broom* groves." Milton uses *brown* repeatedly in the same way. So in *Paradise Lost*, ix. 1088: " Where highest woods spread their umbrage broad and *brown* at evening." The change in the text is strongly opposed by some. I can well understand why a grove should be called *brown*, but not how a growth of *broom* should be called a *grove ;* the broom, or *genista*, being, as Nares observes, a mere shrub, which gives no shade. In support, however, of the old reading, it is said that one kind of broom grows to the height of a tall man. So do some species of corn; yet who would speak of a *grove* of corn? Lettsom comments as follows: "The notion of disconsolate lovers betaking themselves to groves is common enough in poetry: Shakespeare himself has placed Romeo in a sycamore grove when Rosaline was cruel; and we may judge from this the sort of grove he would select for a young gentleman in like case. Till it can be shewn that a growth of broom may be called a grove, it seems idle, to dispute about the height of the shrub. In Babington's *Botany* it is said to be two and a half or three feet high; and this is certainly the usual height to which it grows on Hampstead Heath, though occasionally a plant may be found taller: I am told that in Italy it grows to the height of six or seven feet; but that surely is no great matter. The defences set up for the old reading appear to me singularly weak." I must add that, in the first scene of the play, we have an instance of *broom* evidently misprinted *brown* in the original; and I do not see why *brown* might not as easily have been misprinted *broom*. See note on the passage, page 149.

P. 122. *Earth's increase*, and *foison plenty.* — So the second folio: the first omits *and*. The prefix "*Cer.*" also wanting in the original.

P. 123. *So rare a wonder'd father and a* wife
Make *this place Paradise.* — The original has *wise* for *wife* and *makes* for *make*. The old reading has been stoutly maintained; but I can hardly think that Ferdinand would leave the wife out of such a reckoning, especially the wife being Miranda, or the Wonderful. Then too *wise* and *Paradise* make a disagreeable jingle. See foot-note 25.

P. 123. *You nymphs, call'd Naiads, of the* winding *brooks,*
With your sedge crowns and ever-harmless looks,
Leave your crisp channels, and on this green land
Answer our summons; Juno does command. — In the first of these lines, the original has *windring*, which Rowe corrected to *winding*. Some editors read *wandering*. In the second line, the original has "*sedg'd* crowns." The reading in the text is Walker's, and is also

found in Collier's second folio. It appears that final *d* and final *e* were especially apt to be confounded. In the fourth line, the old text has *your* instead of *our*. Probably repeated by mistake from the line before.

P. 124. *This is* most *strange : your father's in some passion
That works him strongly.* — So Hanmer and Dyce. The original lacks *most*, which certainly helps the sense, and finishes the verse ; still I am not quite sure about it.

P. 124. *You do*, my son, look *in a movèd sort.* — The original reads " You do *look, my son*," &c. The reading in the text was proposed by Seymour.

P. 125. *And, like this insubstantial pageant faded,
Leave not a* rack *behind.* — So the old editions. Dyce and some others print *wreck* instead of *rack ;* and Dyce produces several instances where the form *rack* is clearly used for *wreck*. But I think the sense of *rack* harmonizes best with the context. Thus the expressions, " Melted into thin air," " the baseless fabric of this vision," " shall dissolve," and " this insubstantial pageant faded," naturally draw into the sense of something thinner and more vapoury than is fairly expressed by the word *wreck*. See foot-note 32.

P. 125. Ferd. Mira.   *We wish* you *peace.*
     Pros. [To ARIEL.] *Come with a thought ! — I thank* ye.
     [Exeunt FERD. and MIRA.]— *Ariel, come !* — The original has " wish *your* peace," and " I thank *thee* Ariel: come." The first correction is Walker's, the other Dyce's ; and both seem eminently judicious. See foot-note 34.

P. 126. *Well, say again, where didst thou leave these varlets ?* — The original lacks *Well*.

P. 127.   *On whom my pains,
Humanely taken, all* are *lost, quite lost.* — So Walker. The original has " all, *all* lost." Hanmer reads " *are all* lost."

P. 128. *Nay, good my lord, give me thy favour still.* — The original **\`acks** *Nay*, and thus defeats Caliban of his wonted rhythm.

P. 129.   *Let's along,*
    And do the murder first. — The original has " Let's *alone*." The correction is Theobald's, and I think it needs no defence.

ACT V., SCENE I.

P. 132. *In the same fashion as you gave in charge :*
    Just as you left them ; all are *prisoners, sir,*
    In the line-grove, &c. — In the second of these lines, the old text reads " all prisoners, sir." The Poet could hardly have been so indifferent to rhythm as to leave such a gap. Pope reads " all *your* prisoners." The reading in the text is from Collier's second folio.

P. 132. *And the remainder mourning over them,*
    Brimful of sorrow and dismay ; but chiefly
    He *that you term'd " The good old lord, Gonzalo" :*
    His tears run down his beard, like winter-*drops*
    From eaves of reeds. — In the third of these lines, the original has *Him* for *He*, and inserts *sir* after *term'd*, to the manifest spoiling of the metre. — In the fourth line, again, the old text has " *winters* drops." Corrected in the fourth folio.

P. 134. *And 'twixt the green sea and the* azure *vault*
    Set roaring war. — The original has " *assur'd* vault." See note on " With your *sedge* crowns," page 166.

P. 135. *A solemn air, as the best comforter*
    To an unsettled fancy, cure the brains,
    Now useless, boil'd *within* the *skull!* — In the first of these lines, the old text has *and* instead of *as*. But the latter is clearly required ; for Prospero certainly means that " a solemn air" is itself " the best comforter." Shakespeare is almost classical in his estimate of the power of music ; and here he probably had in mind the effect of David's harp and voice in charming the evil spirit out of King Saul

See 1 Samuel, xvi. 23.— In the second and third lines, again, the original has "cure *thy* brains," and "within *thy* skull." But Prospero is evidently speaking either to all six of the men or else to none of them. If he is speaking to them, it should be *your — your;* if merely in reference to them, it should be either *the — the* or *their — their*. The correction is Dr. C. M. Ingleby's, and is manifestly right; though, for my part, I should prefer *their — their*, but that it involves more of literal change. The old copies have many clear instances of like error. — The original also has *boile* instead of *boil'd*, which the sense naturally requires. Probably the Poet wrote *boild;* and here, as in many other cases, final *d* and final *e* were confounded. See foot-note 10.

P. 135.   *O* thou *good Gonzalo,*
    My true preserver, &c. — So Walker. The original lacks *thou,* and so has an ugly gap in the verse. "O *my* good Gonzalo" is the reading of some editors.

P. 136. *In a cowslip's bell I lie, —*
    There I couch : when owls do cry,
    On the bat's back I do fly
    After Summer *merrily.* — In the second of these lines, I adopt the punctuation proposed by Heath. The original reads "There I couch when owls do cry." Heath notes as follows: "If Ariel 'couches in the cowslip's bell when owls do cry,' it follows that he couches there in Winter; for that, as Mr. Warburton hath shown, from the authority of our Poet himself, as well as from the general notoriety of the fact, is the season when owls do cry. How, then, can it consistently be said, as it is in the words immediately following, that he constantly flies the approach of Winter, by following the Summer in its progress to other climates?" — In the fourth line, Theobald changed *Summer* to *sunset;* plausibly, as it assimilates the meaning to matter of fact. But the Poet ascribes to Ariel and his fellows something of the same qualities which the Fairies have, as delineated in *A Midsummer-Night's Dream.* These beings move entirely according to the pleasure and impulse of their inner nature, unlimited by any external order of facts; "wandering everywhere swifter than the moony sphere," i·

quest of whatever they have most delight in, or most affinity with.
Oberon puts it thus :—

> Then my Queen, in silence sad,
> Trip we after the night's shade:
> We the globe can compass soon,
> Swifter than the wandering Moon.

P. 137.   *The master and the boatswain*

Being awaked, *enforce them to this place.* — So Walker conjectured, and so the context clearly requires. The original has *awake.*
Another instance of *d* and *e* confounded, the Poet having probably
written *awakd.*

P. 138. *But you, my brace of lords, were I so minded,*
I here could pluck his Highness' frown upon you,
And justify you traitors : at this time
I'll tell no tales.
   Sebas. [Aside to ANTO.]   *The Devil speaks in him.*
   Pros.   Now,
For you, most wicked sir, whom to call brother, &c. — In the last
line but one, the original has *No* instead of *Now.* *No* must of course
refer to what Sebastian has just said, "The Devil speaks in him." But
this is evidently spoken either to himself or to his partner in guilt ;
and things so spoken are, I think, never supposed to be heard by the
other persons of the scene. Besides, we naturally want the sense of
now as a transitional word. The correction was proposed by the late
Professor Allen, of Philadelphia.

P. 139. *As great to me, as late ; and,* portable
   To make the dear loss, &c. — The original has *supportable,* which
makes shocking work with the metre. Steevens printed *portable,* which
keeps the sense, saves the verse, and is elsewhere used by the Poet.

P. 140.   *And scarce think*
   Their eyes do offices of truth, these *words*
   Are natural breath. — So Capell. The original has "*their*
words." But Prospero evidently refers to the words himself is speaking. See foot-note 36.

P. 142. *Let us not burden our* remembrance *with*
   A heaviness that's gone. — The original has *remembrances.* Corrected by Pope.

P. 143. When *we, in all* her *trim, freshly beheld*
   Our royal, good, and gallant ship. — The original reads, "*Where* we, in all *our* trim." The last is Thirlby's correction.

P. 145.   *This mis-*shaped *knave, —*
   His mother was a witch. — So Pope and Walker. The original has "mis-*shapen.*"

P. 146. *This is* as strange a thing *as e'er I look'd on.* — The original reads "This is *a strange thing* as," &c. Corrected by Capell.

P. 147. *Where I have hope to see the nuptial*
   Of these our dear-belovèd solemnized. — The original has "our *deere-belov'd solemnized*"; which White and Dyce retain. This, it seems to me, is pushing conservatism one letter too far. It is true, the Poet sometimes has it *solémnizéd;* but then he oftener has it as in the text.

P. 148. *Now my charms are all o'erthrown,* &c. — All Shakespearians, I believe, are pretty much agreed that this Epilogue was not written by Shakespeare. The whole texture and grain of the thing are altogether unlike him. Any one, who will take pains to compare it with the passages of trochaic verse in *A Midsummer-Night's Dream,* must see at once, I think, that the two could not have come from the same hand. It cannot be affirmed with positiveness who did write the Epilogue. As Mr. White observes, such appendages were very apt to be supplied by some second hand; and in Shakespeare's circle of friends and fellow-dramatists there were more than one who might well have done this office for him, either with or without his consent; especially as his plays are known to have passed out of his hands into the keeping of the theatrical company for which he wrote. Both the Prologue and the Epilogue of *King Henry VIII.* have been noted by Johnson and others as decidedly wanting in the right Shakespearian taste.

HIGHER ENGLISH.

(See also Classics for Children, pages 3 to 8.)

Minto's Manual of English Prose Literature.

Designed mainly to show characteristics of style. By WILLIAM MINTO, M.A., Professor of Logic and English Literature in the University of Aberdeen, Scotland. 12mo. Cloth. 566 pages. Mailing Price, $1.65; Introduction, $1.50; Allowance, 40 cents.

THE main design is to assist in directing students in English composition to the merits and defects of our principal writers of prose, enabling them, in some degree at least, to acquire the one and avoid the other. The Introduction analyzes style: elements of style, qualities of style, kinds of composition. Part First gives exhaustive analyses of De Quincey, Macaulay, and Carlyle. These serve as a key to all the other authors treated. Part Second takes up the prose authors in historical order, from the fourteenth century up to the early part of the nineteenth.

H. C. De Motte, *Pres. of Chaddock College, Quincy, Ill.:* We are delighted with it. It is one of the most serviceable books I have seen on the subject. I shall recommend it for our work here. (*Sept. 23, 1886.*)

Hiram Corson, *Prof. of English*

Literature, *Cornell Univ., Ithaca, N.Y.:* Without going outside of this book, an earnest student could get a knowledge of English prose styles, based on the soundest principles of criticism, such as he could not get in any twenty volumes which I know of. (*May 14, 1886.*)

Minto's Characteristics of the English Poets,

from Chaucer to Shirley.

By WILLIAM MINTO, M.A., Professor of Logic and English Literature in the University of Aberdeen, Scotland. 12mo. Cloth. xi + 382 pages. Mailing Price, $1.65; for Introduction, $1.50; Allowance, 40 cents.

THE chief objects of the author are: (1) To bring into clear light the characteristics of the several poets; and (2) to trace how far each was influenced by his literary predecessors and his contemporaries.

Lessons in English.

Adapted to the Study of American Classics. A text-book for High Schools and Academies. By SARA E. H. LOCKWOOD, Teacher of English in the High School. New Haven, Conn. 12mo. Cloth. xix + 403 pages. Mailing Price, $1.25; for introduction, $1.12. Allowance for an old book in exchange, 35 cents.

Thanatopsis and Other Favorite Poems of Bryant.

Prepared especially to accompany Lockwood's Lessons in English. 12mo. Paper. 61 pages. Mailing Price, 12 cents; for introd., 10 cts.

THIS is, in a word, a practical High School text-book of English, embracing language, composition, rhetoric, and literature. It aims to present, in simple and attractive style, the essentials of good English; and, at the same time, to develop a critical literary taste, by applying these technical rules and principles to the study of American Classics.

The plan provides for a course in English extending over the pupil's first year and a half in the High School, the work being preparatory to the study of English Literature as usually pursued in schools of this grade. These "Lessons" include the most important facts concerning the History and Elements of the Language, Common Errors in the Use of English, the Study of Words, Rules for the Construction of Sentences, Figures of Speech, Punctuation, Letter-Writing, Composition, and Biographical Sketches of the seven authors particularly studied, — Irving, Bryant, Longfellow, Whittier, Hawthorne, Holmes, and Lowell.

No other text-book on English includes so much. It is at once a text-book of rhetoric, a hand-book of composition, and an introduction to American literature. A valuable addition to the book will be found in the lists of references given at the close of most of the chapters and after each biographical sketch. These are intended to aid teachers in their preparation of the lessons, and to furnish pupils with additional sources of information.

The work is the outgrowth of years of experience in the schoolroom. The plan has been thoroughly tested, and proved to be a good one. Both teachers and pupils testify that by this plan the study of English is made exceedingly interesting and far more profitable than it was when more theoretical text-books were in use. Teachers will find in the book many valuable exercises and lists of questions, and many helpful suggestions as to methods.

John F. Genung, *Prof. of Rhetoric in Amherst College, and author of "The Practical Elements of Rhetoric":* It is clearly written, concise, with abundant exercises, and taking up the most useful points.

T. Whiting Bancroft, *Prof. of Rhetoric, Brown University, Providence, R.I.:* It successfully solves the problem to give in condensed form an introduction to the study of our American classics. . . . The author's selection of material is wisely made.

Margaret E. Stratton, *Prof. of English and Rhetoric, Wellesley College:* It gives a clear and systematic presentation of the subject, and must greatly facilitate the work of the teacher who lays stress not on formal rules but on the frequent practice of rules, and seeks to give with rules abundant illustration; and what is still more important, tries to awake in young minds a just appreciation of the importance of English through the delightful medium of our best writers.

James E. Thomas, *English High School, Boston:* The best text-book I have thus far seen for the study of English in the high schools.

Harriet O. Nelson, *Teacher of Literature, High School, Haverhill, Mass.:* It seems to me one of the most practical and suggestive works that I have ever seen.

E. W. Boyd, *Head St. Agnes School, Albany, N.Y.:* It is the most satisfactory book of the kind I have ever seen.

Charles McLenegan, *High School, Milwaukee:* The use of the book will be a long step in the right direction. . . . The simplicity and clearness of the book are beautiful. I do not think I ever saw a book of its kind with so little of the dry-as-dust about it.

H. Lee Sellers, *Prin. High School, Galveston:* To my mind it is the very book we have wanted for many years.

George A. Walton, *Agent Massachusetts Board of Education:* It must prove a useful book. The matter and the method are excellent.

Alfred S. Roe, *Prin. High School, Worcester, Mass.:* I have looked the book through carefully, and I can unqualifiedly approve it. I know of nothing better.

J. A. Graves, *Prin. South School, Hartford, Conn.:* I know of no book that seems to me so well adapted to the wants of high schools and academies.

E. J. MacEwan, *Prof. of English, Michigan Agricultural College:* I know of nothing that can compare with it for a two years' course in the public schools, — say last year of grammar grade and first year of high school. I shall be glad to put in a word as occasion offers to help you in getting it into such grades, and in helping grades to get the best thing for themselves at the same time.

H. F. Estill, *Instructor in Language, Sam Houston Normal Institute, Huntsville, Tex.:* In my opinion the book is an admirably clear, compact, and attractive presentation of the essentials of English, and cannot fail to awake in the pupil an appreciation of the strength and beauty of his native tongue, as well as to train him in the art of correct and elegant expression. The chapters on letter-writing and composition are especially good. We ha' decided to introduce it at once the Normal School.

The Practical Elements of Rhetoric.

By JOHN F. GENUNG, Ph.D., Professor of Rhetoric in Amherst College. 12mo. Cloth. xiv + 483 pages. Mailing Price, $1.40; for introduction, $1.25; allowance for an old book in exchange 40 cents.

THE treatment is characterized by : —

1. **Good Sense.** The author, while suitably magnifying his art, recognizes that expression is not a substitute for ideas, that the *how* of speech is secondary to the *what*, that Rhetoric is only means to an end, and that its rules and principles and devices must be employed with caution and good sense.

2. **Simplicity.** Great care has been taken to free the treatment from artificialities. The subjects are most logically ordered, but not too minutely subdivided. So far as possible, terms are used in their popular and usual sense.

3. **Originality.** In a subject so old and so thoroughly studied each new treatment must take large account of what has been done before. This the author has not failed to do. But principally he has made his book from the study of literature at first hand. Traditional principles and rules have been discarded unless found to rest on a basis of truth and practical value.

4. **Availability.** The treatment is throughout *constructive*. The student is regarded at every step as endeavoring to make literature, and is given just what is indispensable to this end. On every point the main problems of construction are stated and solved. Again, the work has been prepared not more in the study than in the classroom, and the adaptation kept constantly in mind of every usage and principle to the actual needs of the actual student.

5. **Completeness.** All of the literary forms have been given something of the fulness hitherto accorded only to argument and oratory. This method is clearly in line with modern requirements. Part I. deals with style; Part II. with invention. All questions arising under both these divisions are fully considered.

6. **Ample Illustration.** Mere precept cannot help seeming arbitrary. In the concrete it bears a different, a more intelligible, and a more convincing look. Accordingly the author has presented no important principle without illustrations drawn from actual usage. It is usage, too, of the best, the most standard writers.

Genung's Rhetoric, though a work on a trite subject, has aroused genuine enthusiasm by its freshness and practical value. Among the many leading institutions that have introduced it are Yale, Wellesley, and Smith Colleges; Cornell, Johns Hopkins, Vanderbilt, and Northwestern Universities; and the Universities of Virginia, North Carolina, Wisconsin, Illinois, Minnesota, Kansas, and Oregon.

C. F. Richardson, *Prof. of English Literature, Dartmouth College, and author of a History of American Literature:* I find it excellent both in plan and execution.

Miss Margaret E. Stratton, *Prof. of Rhetoric, Wellesley College:* The author's treatment of the subject is simple, clear, and sufficiently complete to make his work valuable, whether in the hands of teachers or scholars. There is also a freshness in dealing with rules and precepts which will interest even those students who think rhetoric a dry study. and will help to enliven the task of composition,—the end toward which all teaching of rules should tend.

Miss M. A. Jordan, *Prof. of Rhetoric, Smith College, Northampton, Mass.:* The critic is conscious of a feeling of surprise as he misses the orthodox dulness. The analysis of topics is clear, the illustrations are pertinent and of value in themselves, the rules are concise and portable.

O. L. Elliott, *Instructor in English, Cornell Univ., Ithaca, N.Y.:* I am greatly pleased with the book, and am using it in my classes with every promise of good results. The author seems to have broken completely away from the bad traditions which have filled our rhetorics with absurd rules and absurder examples. There is a freshness, vigor, and quiet good sense in both spirit and method that must, I think, commend the book to all teachers of English.

T. W. Hunt, *Prof. of English Literature, Princeton College, Princeton, N.J.:* It impresses me as a philosophic and useful manual. I like especially its literary spirit.

Jas. M. Garnett, *Prof. of English, University of Virginia:* I have carefully read the whole of it, and am determined to introduce it at once into my class. It suits me better than any other text-book of rhetoric that I have examined.

Charles H. Payne, *Pres. of Ohio Wesleyan University, Delaware, O.:* I have no hesitation in pronouncing it a work of rare excellence. It certainly combines, in a most felicitous way, those qualities claimed for it by the publishers,—good sense, simplicity, originality, availability, completeness, and ample illustration.

W. M. Baskervill, *Prof. of English, Vanderbilt University:* I found it, according to my opinion, the best practical work on the subject now offered for use in America. I shall adopt it next year. It is new and it is fresh, — a good deal to say about a work on so hackneyed a subject.

W. H. Magruder, *Prof. of English, Agricultural and Mechanical College of Mississippi:* For clearness of thought, lucidity of expression, aptness of illustration, — in shor for real teaching power, — I h never seen this work equalled.

Hudson's Expurgated Shakespeare.

For Schools, Clubs, and Families. Revised and enlarged Editions of twenty-three Plays. Carefully expurgated, with Explanatory Notes at the bottom of the page, and Critical Notes at the end of each volume. By H. N. HUDSON, LL.D., Editor of *The Harvard Shakespeare*. One play in each volume. Square 16mo. Varying in size from 128-253 pages. Mailing Price of each: Cloth, 50 cents; Paper, 35 cents. Introduction Price: Cloth, 45 cents; Paper, 30 cents. Per set (in box), $12.00. (To Teachers, $10.00.)

SOME of the special features of this edition are the convenient size and shape of the volumes; the clear type, superior press-work, and attractive binding; the ample introductions; the explanatory notes, easily found at the foot of the page; the critical notes for special study; the judicious expurgation, never mangling either style or story; the acute and sympathetic criticism that has come to be associated with Dr. HUDSON's name; and, finally, the reasonableness of the price.

Oliver Wendell Holmes: An edition of any play of Shakespeare's to which Mr. Hudson's name is affixed does not need a line from anybody to commend it.

Cyrus Northrop, *Prof. of English Literature, Yale College*: They are convenient in form and edited by Hudson, — two good things which I can see at a glance.

Hiram Corson, *Prof. of Rhet. and Eng. Lit., Cornell University*: I consider them altogether excellent. The notes give all the aid needed for an understanding of the text, without waste and distraction of the student's mind. The introductory matter to the several plays is especially worthy of approbation. (*Jan.* 28, 1887.)

C. F. P. Bancroft, *Prin. of Phillips Academy, Andover, Mass.*: Mr. Hudson's appreciation of Shakespeare amounted to genius. His editing accordingly exhibits more than learning and industry. —it reveals insight, sympathy, and conviction. He leads the pupil into the very mind and heart of "the thousand-souled Shakespeare."

Byron Groce, *Master in Public Latin School, Boston*: The amended text is satisfactory; the typography is excellent; the notes are brief, always helpful, not too numerous, and put where they will do the most good; the introductions are vigorous, inspiriting, keenly and soundly critical, and very attractive to boys, especially on account of their directness and warmth, for all boys like enthusiasm. (*Jan.* 22, 1887.)

C. T. Winchester, *Prof. of English, Wesleyan University*: The notes and comments in the school edition are admirably fitted to the need of the student, removing his difficulties by stimulating his interest and quickening his perception. (*Feb.* 10, 1887.)

A. C. Perkins, *Prin. of Adelphi Academy, Brooklyn*: In the preparation of the School Shakespeare, Mr. Hudson met fully the capacities and needs of students in our schools and colleges. (*Feb.* 4, 1887.)

The series consists of the twenty-three plays enumerated below

We furnish of the Old Edition, in paper covers, the plays starred in the following list (Mailing Price, 20 cents ; Introduction, 15 cents):—

*A Midsummer-Night's Dream.³
*The Merchant of Venice.¹
*Much Ado About Nothing
*As You Like It.¹
Twelfth Night.¹
*The Tempest.³
The Winter's Tale.³
King John.
Richard Second.
Richard Third.³
*Henry Fourth, Part First.¹
Henry Fourth, Part Second.¹

*Henry the Fifth.³
*Henry the Eighth.³
*Romeo and Juliet.³
*Julius Cæsar.¹
*Hamlet.¹
*King Lear.³
*Macbeth.³
Antony and Cleopatra.³
*Othello.³
Cymbeline.³
*Coriolanus.³

Hudson's Three-Volume Shakespeare.

For Schools, Families, and Clubs. With Introductions and Notes on each Play. 12mo. Cloth. 636–678 pages per volume. Mailing Price, per volume, $1.40; Introduction, $1.25.

The plays included in the three volumes respectively are indicated by figures in the above list.

The Harvard Edition of Shakespeare's Complete

Works.

By HENRY N. HUDSON, LL.D., Author of the *Life, Art, and Characters of Shakespeare*, Editor of *School Shakespeare*, etc. In *Twenty Volumes*; 12mo ; two plays in each volume ; also in *Ten Volumes*, of four plays each.

RETAIL PRICES.

Twenty-vol. edition, cloth . $35.00	Ten-vol. edition, cloth . . $30.00
Half-calf 55.00	Half-calf 40.00

☞ *Buyers should be careful in ordering not to confound the Harvard Shakespeare with an Old Edition made in 1851, and sold under another name.*

THIS is pre-eminently the edition for libraries, students, an general readers. The type, paper, and binding are attractiv and superior, and the notes represent the editor's rinest thought

An obvious merit of this edition is, that each volume has two sets of notes; one mainly devoted to explaining the text, and placed at the foot of the page; the other mostly occupied with matters of textual comment and criticism, and printed at the end of each play. This arrangement is particularly suited to the convenience of the general student, who does not wish to hunt for an explanation; and to the wants of the special student, who desires extended discussion of a difficulty.

E. P. Whipple, *The Noted Critic :* Hudson's is the most thoughtful and intelligent interpretative criticism which has, during the present century, been written, either in English or German.

N. Y. Evening Express: The most satisfactory and complete edition we have.

N. Y. Tribune: As an interpreter of Shakespeare, imbued with the vital essence of the great English dramatist, and equally qualified by insight and study to penetrate the deepest significance of his writings, it would be difficult to name an English or American scholar who can be compared with the editor of this edition.

Hudson's Life, Art, and Characters of Shake-

speare (Revised Edition, 1882).

By HENRY N. HUDSON, LL.D., Editor of *The Harvard Shakespeare*, etc. In 2 vols. 12mo. 1003 pages. Uniform in size with *The Harvard Shakespeare*, and matches it in the following bindings :—

Cloth . . . . Retail Price, $4.00 per set.
Half-calf . . . . . . " " 8.00 "

THESE two volumes contain : *The Life of Shakespeare; An Historical Sketch of the Origin and Growth of the Drama in England; Shakespeare's Contemporaries; Shakespeare's Art,* discussing under this head, Nature and Use of Art, Principles of Art, Dramatic Composition, Characterization, Humour, Style, Moral Spirit; *Shakespeare's Characters,* containing critical discourses on twenty-five of the Plays.

London Athenæum: They deserve to find a place in every library devoted to Shakespeare, to editions of his works, to his biography, or to the works of commentators.

Hudson's Classical English Reader.

For High Schools, Academies, and the upper grades of Grammar Schools. 12mo. Cloth. 467 pages. Mailing Price, $1.10; Introduction, $1.00; Allowance for old book in use, 30 cents.

IT contains selections from Bryant, Burke, Burns, Byron, Carlyle, Coleridge, Cowley, Cowper, Dana, Froude, Gladstone, Goldsmith, Gray, Helps, Herbert, Hooker, Hume, Irving, Keble, Lamb, Landor, Longfellow, Macaulay, Milton, Peabody, Scott, Shakespeare, Southey, Spenser, Talfourd, Taylor, Webster, Whittier, Wordsworth, and other standard authors, with explanatory and critical foot-notes. This is a book that seems to merit a place in every school of advanced grade below the college.

F. J. Child, *Prof. of English in Harvard University:* A boy who knew this book as well as boys who are good for anything generally know their readers, might almost be said to be liberally educated.

Essays on Education, English Studies, and Shakespeare.

By HENRY N. HUDSON, LL.D., *the Eminent Shakespearian.* Square 16mo. Paper. 118 pages. Mailing Price, 25 cents.

THE volume contains: The Preface to the new edition of *Hamlet*, An Essay on "*English in Schools*," "*Shakespeare as a Text-Book*," "*How to Use Shakespeare in Schools.*"

Hudson's Text-Book of Poetry.

By H. N. HUDSON, LL.D. 12mo. Cloth. 704 pages. Mailing Price, $1.40; Introduction, $1.25.

SELECTIONS from Wordsworth, Coleridge, Burns, Beattie, Goldsmith, and Thomson. With sketches of the authors lives, and instructive foot-notes, historical and explanatory.

Hudson's Text-Book of Prose.

By H. N. HUDSON, LL.D. 12mo. Cloth. 648 pages. Mailing Price, $1.40; Introduction, $1.25.

FROM Burke, Webster, and Bacon. With sketches of the authors' lives, and foot-notes, historical and explanatory.

Hudson's Selections of Prose and Poetry.

Annotated. 12mo. Paper. Mailing Price of each, 20 cents; Introduction Price, 15 cents.

Edmund Burke. SECTION 1. Five Speeches and ten Papers. SECTION 2. A Sketch of his Life. *A Letter to a Noble Lord*, and eleven extracts.

Daniel Webster. SECTION 1. The *Reply to Hayne*, and six extracts. SECTION 2. A Sketch of his Life, and extracts from twenty-five Speeches.

Lord Bacon. A Sketch of his Life, and extracts from thirty Essays.

Wordsworth. SECTION I. Life of Wordsworth, the Prelude, and thirty-three Poems. SECTION II. Sixty Poems and Sonnets, accompanied by foot-notes, historical and explanatory.

Coleridge and Burns. Biographies of the Poets, and forty-five Poems.

Addison and Goldsmith. A Life of each, fifteen Papers from Addison, and eleven Prose Selections from Goldsmith, with *The Deserted Village.*

Craik's English of Shakespeare.

Illustrated in a Philological Commentary on Julius Cæsar. By GEORGE L. CRAIK, Queen's College, Belfast. Edited, from the third revised London edition, by W. J. ROLFE. Cambridge, Mass. 12mo. Cloth. 400 pages. Mailing Price, $1.00; Introduction, 90 cents.

AN exposition in regard both to the language or style of Shakespeare, and to the English language generally.

Shakspere's Versification.

Notes on Shakspere's Versification, with Appendix on the Verse Tests, and a short Descriptive Bibliography. By GEORGE H. BROWNE, A.M. 12mo. Paper. 34 pages. Price, interleaved, 25 cents.

Shakespeare and Chaucer Examinations.

Edited, with some remarks on the "Class-Room Study of Shakespeare," by WILLIAM TAYLOR THOM, M.A., Professor of English in Hollins Institute, Va. Square 16mo. Cloth. 346 pages. Mailing Price, $1.10; for introduction, $1.00.

THIS is a revised and enlarged edition of the *Two Shakespeare Examinations*, published several years and very much liked by teachers of English Literature. That book contained two examinations held at Hollins Institute in 1881, on *Hamlet;* in 1882, on *Macbeth,* for the annual prize by the *New Shakespeare Society* of England. Besides these, there are in the new edition the Examinations on *King Lear* (1883), on *Othello* (1884), on *The Merchant of Venice* (1886); a Chaucer Examination (1886), set chiefly by Professor Child, of Harvard University, and based upon the "Prologue," "The Knight's Tale," and the "Nun's Priest's Tale" of the *Canterbury Tales;* with some additional remarks on the Study of Shakespeare and references to the *Tempest.*

W. M. Baskervill, *Prof. in Vanderbilt University:* We heartily recommend these examinations to teachers. They are full of suggestive information. They will serve as admirable models.

Introduction to the Poetry of Robert Browning.

By WILLIAM JOHN ALEXANDER, Ph.D., Munro Professor of the English Language and Literature, Dalhousie College and University, Halifax, N.S.. and formerly Fellow of Johns Hopkins University. 12mo. Cloth. v + 212 pages. Mailing Price, $1.10; for introduction, $1.00.

THE book opens with an account of Browning's most striking peculiarities in method and style, and attempts to find an explanation of these in the conditions amidst which the Poet has worked, and in the nature of the themes which he treats. In the next place, an exposition is given of those general ideas pervading his work, which can only be gathered from the study of many of his poems, and yet are needful for the full understanding of almost any one of them. This exposition is contained in a series of chapters treating of "Browning's Philosophy," "Christianity as Presented in Browning's Works," and "Browning's Theory of Art." These chapters are followed by a brief chronological review of his writings, and characterization of his development. The various points treated throughout the Introduction are illustrated by a series of selected poems, furnished with careful analyses and copious critical comments. It is hoped that by thus unfolding, in a few typical examples, the characteristics and merits of Browning, the reader may at once be enabled to acquire a real knowledge of his poetry, and be prepared for further unassisted study of his work. Attention is especially directed to the Analysis of Sordell much fuller and more exact, it is believed, than any heretof published.

Arnold's English Literature.

Historical and Critical.

With an Appendix on English Metres, and Summaries of the Different
Literary Periods. By THOMAS ARNOLD, M.A., of University College,
Oxford. American edition. Revised. 12mo. Cloth. 558 pages. Mailing Price, $1.65; Introduction (with or without the following pamphlet),
$1.50; Allowance for old book, 40 cents.
The Anglo-Saxon and Norman Periods have been republished, from
the fourth revised English edition, and can be furnished in paper binding. Mailing Price, 30 cents; Introduction, 25 cents.

THE student of this manual will receive just impressions of the
relative value of names and books, as well as political and religious influences. Indeed, the adjustment and arrangement of material are managed with wonderful dexterity and analytic clearness.

H. H. Morgan, *Prin. of High* that of the student; for he would
School, St. Louis, Mo.: I should find much which could otherwise
most fully recommend it to any be obtained only by extensive read-
one whose interest in literature was ing.

First Two Books of Milton's Paradise Lost;

and Milton's Lycidas.

By HOMER B. SPRAGUE, Ph.D., formerly Principal of the Girls' High
School, Boston. 12mo. Cloth. 198 pages. Mailing Price, 55 cents; Introduction, 45 cents.

THIS edition furnishes convenient and suggestive notes, with
excellent type and arrangement, and presents an approved
formula for conducting class exercises. It omits fifteen or twenty
objectionable lines.

William F. Warren, *President of* me admirably adapted to its pur-
Boston University : It seems to pose.

A Hand-Book of Poetics.

For Students of English Verse. By FRANCIS B. GUMMERE, Ph.D.,
Head Master of the Swain Free School, New Bedford, Mass., and formerly Instructor in English in Harvard College. 12mo. Cloth. x + 250
pages. Mailing Price, $1.10; for Introduction, $1.00.

THE book has three divisions, — Subject-Matter, Style, Metre.
Each is treated from two points of view, — the historical, trac-
ng the growth of different kinds of subject, of expression, or of

rhythm; and the theoretical, stating clearly the principles and laws of the matter discussed.

F. A. March, *Prof. of English Literature, Lafayette College:* An excellent book: a work of good sense and good taste, and much learning in small compass.

J. M. Garnett, *Prof. of English Literature, University of Virginia:* It has fulfilled my anticipations, and it supplies a real deficiency in text-books. I do not know, anywhere in English, of a better treatment of the subject.

F. J. Child, *Prof. of English, Harvard College:* I think you have an exceedingly fine book in Mr. Gummere's Poetics.

Outlines of the Art of Expression.

By J. H. GILMORE, Professor of Logic, Rhetoric, and English, in the University of Rochester, N.Y. 12mo. Cloth. 117 pages. Mailing Price, 65 cents; Introduction, 60 cents.

A TREATISE on English Composition and Rhetoric, designed especially for Academies, High Schools, and the Freshman Class in Colleges.

Fulton and Trueblood's Choice Readings.

From Popular and Standard Authors.

Compiled and arranged by ROBERT I. FULTON and THOMAS C. TRUEBLOOD, Associate Founders and Directors of the University School of Oratory, Kansas City, Mo., and Teachers of Elocution in the Univ. of Mich., the Ohio Wesleyan Univ., the Kentucky Univ., and the Missouri State Univ. 12mo. 729 pages. By Mail, $1.65; Introduction, $1.50. *Presentation edition,* stamped cover, full gilt, fine paper, $4.00 *retail.*

ITS distinctive feature is the number, variety, and interest of the pieces, classified according to their character, and covering the entire range of available selections. Indices are given to the best scenes from all the plays of Shakespeare, 139 choice readings from the Bible, and 159 hymns, — all classified. A complete diagram of the principles of vocal expression is added.

J. W. Churchill, *Prof. of Elocution, Theological Seminary, Andover, Mass.:* The excellent purpose of the authors has been very successfully accomplished, both in the expository and illustrative material. The selections are interesting—sometimes through novelty, but more often because of their intrinsic worth.

Wm. B. Chamberlain, *Instructor in Elocution, Oberlin College, O.:* They *are choice* indeed. I think I do not know of any collection representing so many good authors and so well arranged. The indices, especially that to scenes from Shakespeare, form a very valuable addition to the volume. (*June 11, 1885.*)

Fulton & Trueblood's Chart.

Illustrating the Principles of Vocal Expression.

By ROBERT I. FULTON & T. C. TRUEBLOOD, compilers of Fulton & Trueblood's Choice Readings. Printed on extra tough paper, 36 × 60 inches, bound on the edges, and mounted. Retail price, $2.00. Special introduction terms on application.

THE chart presents a complete system of vocal culture and elocution at a glance, thus avoiding the necessity of turning the leaves of a book or a series of charts. The principles are scientifically arranged and supplemented with diagrams, exercises, and illustrative sentences.

The chart is recommended to professional elocutionists, no matter what school or system they represent; to all students of vocal culture and expression, as an invaluable aid in private practice, suggesting a regular, systematic, and judicious drill — the most imperative condition of success; and to the teachers in the public schools, enabling them to develop the voices of children and impress upon them the principles of correct expression.

F. H. Sargent, *Prin. New York School of Acting:* I find it an exceedingly good exposition of the Rush system of voice training. I shall be glad to recommend it as I have opportunity. (*Jan.* 14, 1888.)

A Method of English Composition.

By T. WHITING BANCROFT, Professor of Rhetoric and English Literature in Brown University. 12mo. Cloth. 101 pages. Mailing Price, 55 cents; Introduction Price, 50 cents; Allowance, 18 cents.

THE author's intention is to furnish to colleges, academies, and high schools a brief system of instruction in the preparation of essays or compositions. The second part consists of lists of classified themes, with specimens of plans of compositions, etc.

E. E. Smith, *Prof. of English and History, Purdue University, Lafayette, Ind.:* I have used it with an advanced class to decided advantage. The divisions and the suggestive arrangement of the various kinds of subjects that may be treated in essays, orations, and debates, is such, I found, as to remove unnecessary obstacles, and at the same time to require thought on the student's part.

Lee's Graphic Chart of English Literature.

By Y. P. LEE, of Yale College. Printed on tough manilla paper 24 × 39 inches in size. Mailing Price, 30 cents; for introduction, 25 cents.

CLASSICS FOR CHILDREN.

Choice Literature; Full Notes; Large Type; Firm Binding; Low Prices.

Each of the volumes is printed in large type, on good paper, and firmly bound. Each is complete; or abridged, where cutting has been necessary, by a skilful hand, without impairment of style or story. Illustrations, when desirable, are freely used. Illustrated books are indicated by stars. The prices have been made as low as possible. An edition has been bound in cloth, omitting the headline "Classics for Children." The books may be had in sets, boxed.

Hans Andersen's Fairy Tales.
 *FIRST SERIES: Supplementary to the Third Reader.
 *SECOND SERIES: Supplementary to the Fourth Reader.
*Æsop's Fables, with selections from Krilof and La Fontaine.
*Kingsley's Water-Babies: A Story for a Land Baby.
*Ruskin's King of the Golden River: A Legend of Stiria.
*The Swiss Family Robinson. Abridged.
Robinson Crusoe. Concluding with his departure from the island.
*Kingsley's Greek Heroes.
Lamb's Tales from Shakespeare. "Meas. for Meas." omitted.
Scott's Tales of a Grandfather.
*Martineau's Peasant and Prince.
Scott's Lady of the Lake.
Scott's Lay of the Last Minstrel.
Lamb's Adventures of Ulysses.
Church's Stories of the Old World.
Scott's Talisman. Complete.
Scott's Quentin Durward. Slightly abridged.
Irving's Sketch Book. Six selections, including "Rip Van Winkle."
Shakespeare's Merchant of Venice.
Scott's Guy Mannering. Complete.
Scott's Ivanhoe. Complete.   Scott's Rob Roy. Complete.
Johnson's Rasselas: Prince of Abyssinia.
Gulliver's Travels. The Voyages to Lilliput and Brobdingnag.
*Plutarch's Lives. From Clough's Translation.
Goldsmith's Vicar of Wakefield.
Hale's Arabian Nights.

GINN & COMPANY, Publishers,
BOSTON, NEW YORK, AND CHICAGO.

BOOKS ON ENGLISH LITERATURE.

Allen	Reader's Guide to English History	$ .25
Arnold . . .	English Literature	1.50
Bancroft . .	A Method of English Composition	.50
Browne . .	Shakespere Versification	.25
Fulton & Trueblood: Choice Readings	1.50
	Chart Illustrating Principles of Vocal Expression,	2.00
Genung . .	Practical Elements of Rhetoric	1.25
Gilmore . .	Outlines of the Art of Expression	.60
Ginn	Scott's Lady of the Lake . . . *Bds.*, .35 ; *Cloth*, .50
	Scott's Tales of a Grandfather . *Bds.*, .40 ; *Cloth*, .50
Gummere .	Handbook of Poetics	1.00
Hudson . .	Harvard Edition of Shakespeare : —
	20 Vol. Edition. *Cloth, retail* 25.00
	10 Vol. Edition. *Cloth, retail* 20.00
	Life, Art, and Character of Shakespeare. 2 vols.
	Cloth, retail	4.00
	New School Shakespeare. *Cloth.* Each Play .	.45
	Old School Shakespeare, per play	.20
	Expurgated Family Shakespeare	10.00
	Essays on Education, English Studies, etc. . .	.25
	Three Volume Shakespeare, per vol.	1.25
	Text-Book of Poetry	1.25
	Text-Book of Prose	1.25
	Pamphlet Selections, Prose and Poetry . . .	.15
	Classical English Reader	1.00
Johnson . .	Rasselas . . . . *Bds.*, .30 ; *Cloth*, .40
Lee	Graphic Chart of English Literature	.25
Martineau .	The Peasant and the Prince . *Bds.*, .35 ; *Cloth*, .50
Minto . . .	Manual of English Prose Literature	1.50
	Characteristics of English Poets	2.00
Rolfe	Craik's English of Shakespeare	.90
Scott . . .	Guy Mannering . . . . . *Bds.*, .60 ; *Cloth*, .75
	Ivanhoe . . . . *Bds.*, .60 ; *Cloth*, .75
	Talisman . . . . *Bds.*, .50 ; *Cloth*, .60
	Rob Roy . . . . *Bds.*, .60 ; *Cloth*, .75
Sprague .	Milton's Paradise Lost, and Lycidas	.45
	Six Selections from Irving's Sketch-Book
	Bds., .25 ; *Cloth*, .35
Swift . . .	Gulliver's Travels . . . . *Bds.*, .30 ; *Cloth*, .40
Thom	Shakespeare and Chaucer Examinations . . .	.00

GINN & COMPANY'S

ANNOTATED ENGLISH CLASSICS

GINN & COMPANY'S
ANNOTATED ENGLISH CLASSICS.

Edited by H. N. HUDSON, LL.D.

Shakespeare's

Hamlet.	Othello.
Macbeth.	Cymbeline.
King Lear.	King John.
The Tempest.	Coriolanus.
Julius Cæsar.	Twelfth Night.
As You Like It.	Richard Third.
Richard Second.	Henry the Fifth.
Romeo and Juliet.	Henry the Eighth.
Antony and Cleopatra.	The Winter's Tale.
The Merchant of Venice.	Henry IV., Part First.
Much Ado About Nothing.	Henry IV., Part Second.

A Midsummer-Night's Dream.

Pamphlet Selections of Prose and Poetry.

No. I. Edmund Burke.	No. V. Lord Bacon.
II. Edmund Burke.	VI. William Wordsworth.
III. Daniel Webster.	VII. Coleridge and Burns.
IV. Daniel Webster.	VIII. Addison and Goldsmith.

Edited by HOMER B. SPRAGUE, Ph.D.

Two Books of Milton's Paradise Lost, and Lycidas.
Six Selections from Irving's Sketch-Book.